Still Running

Still Running

My Life as the First Black Football Player in the SEC

Nathaniel Northington

Foreword by Gerald L. Smith
Afterword by La Monte McNeese

 UNIVERSITY PRESS OF KENTUCKY

A note to the reader: One of the quotations printed in this volume contains a racial slur. The original terminology is included to provide full historical context for the events under discussion. Discretion is advised.

2024 expanded edition published by The University Press of Kentucky

Scholarly publisher for the Commonwealth, serving Bellarmine University, Berea College, Centre College of Kentucky, Eastern Kentucky University, The Filson Historical Society, Georgetown College, Kentucky Historical Society, Kentucky State University, Morehead State University, Murray State University, Northern Kentucky University, Spalding University, Transylvania University, University of Kentucky, University of Louisville, University of Pikeville, and Western Kentucky University.

Editorial and Sales Offices: The University Press of Kentucky
663 South Limestone Street, Lexington, Kentucky 40508–4008
www.kentuckypress.com

Scripture quotations are from the King James Version (KJV) of the Holy Bible. Scripture quotations marked (NKJV) are taken from the New King James Version, © 1979, 1980, 1982, 1984 by Thomas Nelson, Inc. Used by permission. All rights reserved.

Cataloging-in-Publication data for a previous edition of this book is available at the Library of Congress: https://lccn.loc.gov/2013443986

ISBN 978-0-8131-9831-6 (hardcover)
ISBN 978-0-8131-9815-6 (paperback)
ISBN 978-0-8131-9816-3 (pdf)
ISBN 978-0-8131-9817-0 (epub)

This book is printed on acid-free paper meeting the requirements of the American National Standard for Permanence in Paper for Printed Library Materials.

Manufactured in the United States of America.

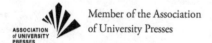
Member of the Association
of University Presses

To Mom and Dad, who loved me and trained me in the way
I should go—"in the fear and admonition of the Lord."
To Renee and Nate Jr., with all my love.

To my circle of strong friends in the neighborhood who always had
my back—especially my best friend, Will, and the Seay family.

To Greg Page, Wilbur Hackett, Houston Hogg, and Albert Johnson,
my fellow pioneers.

❧

And to the love of my life:
Gwendolyn, who loved me dearly and who taught me how to love.
I will see you again in heaven.

Contents

Foreword

On December 19, 1965, Nate Northington became the first African American athlete to sign a scholarship to play football at the University of Kentucky (UK) and in the Southeastern Conference (SEC). When the 1966 fall season began, he and Greg Page were the only two African Americans on the freshman football rooster. The 1967 edition of *UK Football Facts* described Northington, a Louisville resident, as being "so fast and agile that he covers five yards in two strides. . . . The slender Negro, who gives every indication of future stardom, is classed as having a fine temperament and easily coachable." Page was listed as a "rangy young Negro. . . . Excellent range and quickness . . ., One of the strongest men on the team." While both had successful seasons, Page did not live to compete with the UK varsity football team. His death in the fall of 1967 was tragic, controversial, and terribly painful for all who knew him.

Page and Northington were extremely close friends. When they signed with UK, national headlines featured stories on civil rights protests, urban uprisings, and the Vietnam War. Black Kentuckians were still actively pursuing racial equality in employment, housing, and education. Meanwhile, several institutions of higher learning had begun to eliminate the color line in their athletic programs. The Big Eight, Big Ten, and Missouri Valley Conference were signing Black players soon after World War II. By 1964, several of Kentucky's institutions had signed African American athletes. White students were an instrumental voice in the UK Athletic Association's decision to integrate its athletic programs in May 1963.

A few days after Northington signed with UK, President John W. Oswald wrote to a 1922 UK alum who had lobbied support for the new policy: "We have been successful in signing our first Negro athlete and look forward to many others now that the ice has been broken." Kentucky governor Ned Breathitt was equally pleased with Northington's decision to come to UK. After all, he had played an integral role in selling the opportunity to Northington. He personally felt "a heavy responsibility" for Northington's complete safety (Gerald L. Smith, "'Give *"Us"* Something to Yell For!': Athletics and the Black Campus Movement at the University of Kentucky, 1965–1969," in *Slavery and Freedom in the Bluegrass State: Revisiting My Old Kentucky Home*, ed. Gerald L. Smith [Lexington: University Press of Kentucky, 2023]). In January 1966, Breathitt signed the Kentucky Civil Rights Act in the state capitol. However, once Northington arrived on campus, he would not meet with the governor again for more than twenty years. He finally did during a UK Board of Trustees meeting when he and Greg were recognized as the first Black players.

In 1999, the University of Kentucky commemorated the fiftieth anniversary of the first admittance of Black people to the institution. I was the director of the African American Studies and Research Program at the time. I organized a panel discussion titled "Playing Black and Blue: UK and the African American Athlete." I invited individuals from different sports to participate on the panel. I wanted each player to tell their story of playing at UK. I informed a reporter writing a story about the program that it was intended to "serve as an insightful educational experience for all seeking to reconcile the past with the present." But Nate Northington was not ready to tell his story. Over the years, he had become hesitant to do interviews because the media tended to take his comments out of context.

I was delighted to see the first edition of his book in 2013. Written with LaMonte McNeese, it is about faith, family, friends, and football. Northington takes readers on an inspiring journey that offers memories of the Black community of Newburg in Louisville during the early 1960s. He provides interesting stories about the basketball and football games he competed in against neighborhood friends, which included the late great Hall of Fame basketball player Wes Unseld. He offers intriguing details of his recruitment to UK. The book captures his thoughts about his coaches, his teammates, and the campus community.

Page's death was tragic. It occurred at a time when Black people were skeptical about attending the university. Northington shares insight into the controversy and rumors surrounding the event. He gives a candid reflection on the pressures he faced and the physical and emotional pain he endured after the death of his dear friend. Moreover, he explains his decision to leave UK and finish his football career and college education at Western Kentucky University. In 1970, he won an Ohio Valley Conference (OVC) championship, was recognized as the team's most valued player, and was selected to the All-OVC second team.

The SEC has never been the same since Nate Northington signed with UK. In the fall of 1967, in an opening game against Indiana University, he became the first Black SEC football player to compete against a Big Ten school. On September 30, 1967, he became the first to play in an SEC game. His playing time that day against Ole Miss was limited to less than four minutes because of a recurring shoulder injury. But his presence on the field signaled the arrival of life-changing opportunities for generations of Black football players. They now occupy a commanding presence on the offensive and defensive line of scrimmage. They have won championships and Heisman Trophies. They can acquire financial success while being in school because of the name, image, and likeness policy for college athletes.

In recent years, Northington has deservedly received wide recognition for his place in the history of SEC and college football. This updated edition of his book captures his reflections on all the attention he has received. It is ironic that the University of Mississippi was the first institution to name an award in his honor. Following the first edition of this book, the university's athletics department and the William Winter Institute for Racial Reconciliation established the Nathaniel Northington Groundbreaker in Athletics Award. It is bestowed on a student athlete who is committed to racial reconciliation and who excels in athletics, leadership, scholarship, and citizenship. Northington was the first honoree. And, in further appreciation for his pioneering role, the school purchased copies of his book for its athletes.

Regrettably, many SEC players are still unfamiliar with Northington's courageous role in integrating athletic competition. He changed and challenged the course of SEC football with humility, dignity, and an unconquerable spirit. In his heart, he still misses Greg Page. They came to UK together, played together, and lived together as student athletes. They were "brothers." As a Christian minister, Northington accentuates the sovereignty and grace of God throughout this book. It is his testimony, and he tells it well. And, like many others, I am so glad he did.

Gerald L. Smith

Introduction

I remain appreciative for the tremendous recognition I have received since the first edition of my memoir was published in 2013. For nearly fifty years, I struggled to write my story of integrating the Southeastern Conference (SEC) athletic league. After reading sports magazine articles and viewing documentaries, I realized it was time for me to share my thoughts and experiences in my own words. Most importantly, I believed that God wanted me to tell my story.

Once my book was published, I began a relatively conservative book-signing tour, starting on a local level but later expanding to other Kentucky cities. I was shocked when I learned the University of Mississippi's Athletics Department and the William Winter Institute for Racial Reconciliation wanted to honor me by establishing an award in my name. I listened to the message two or three times to ensure I was hearing the message correctly. It was hard for me to comprehend that Ole Miss would recognize me in such a special way. The Nathaniel Northington Groundbreaker in Athletics Award would be given annually to an Ole Miss student athlete who had distinguished him- or herself in athletics, leadership, scholarship, or citizenship and served as a trailblazer for racial reconciliation. As the first African American to integrate the SEC, I was the first recipient of the award. The university went even further by purchasing copies of my book for all the players.

In 2014, Blake Berson, a producer with the CBS Sports Network, wanted to speak with me about a proposed documentary about my experience integrating SEC football. Initially I was reluctant, given that other documentaries had focused on the University of Kentucky's all-white basketball team instead of recognizing the positive achievement I'd made in the mid-1960s. The movie *Glory Road* told the story of Texas Western's 1966 all-Black starting five, who led the team in defeating Kentucky in the National Collegiate Athletic Association (NCAA) championship basketball game. However, the movie failed to mention that I had already accepted a football scholarship to integrate athletics at the University of Kentucky (UK) and in the SEC.

After meeting with Blake, I was impressed with his genuine interest in presenting my perspective, and so I agreed to partner with him to tell my story. Finally, my story would be shown in a documentary format, and those persons at UK responsible for integrating the athletic program would receive proper recognition. I was extremely satisfied with the 2015 release of *Forward Progress: The Integration of SEC Football.* CBS News legal analyst Jack Ford served as executive producer. The initial screening took place at the Muhammad Ali Center in Louisville on February 12, 2015.

Over three hundred guests were present, including Louisville mayor Greg Fischer and many other dignitaries. Many of my family members attended, including my children, and so did many of my coworkers and some of my teammates, including two of my fellow UK trailblazers who were also included in the film, Wilbur Hackett and Houston Hogg. I was excited during the reception and enjoyed participating in the panel discussion after the screening. The documentary debuted on CBS Sports Network on Monday, February 16, 2015, during Black History Month.

In June of that year, I was inducted into the UK Athletics Hall of Fame. I had never imagined that; it was the last thing on my mind. What a tremendous honor. I noted in my speech "that when Greg Page and I came here to Lexington and suited up and walked on that practice field for the first time, we felt ten feet tall and larger than life. We were so proud. Not because we felt we were doing anything great but just because we were living out our dreams of playing major college football—the game that we loved so much and that we loved to play. We were just two teenagers from different parts of the Commonwealth who were coming to college and living out our dreams."

I will never forget 2015; it was a memorable and bittersweet year. Five days after the debut of *Forward Progress*, my mother went home to be with the Lord Jesus Christ. Our beloved mother, who had lived her entire life as a spiritual saint of God, who had loved us with her whole heart, had now transitioned home to heaven. Although my family and I mourned her departure, we did not sorrow as do those who have no hope. We loved her, and we realized she had gone to a better place, so we rejoiced at her homegoing. I will always believe she waited until the national showing of my story before she passed. God's timing is perfect. Although Mom did not have the opportunity to view the documentary, I believe that God allowed her to live until it had aired on television. It felt as though she was right there viewing it with us. I could feel and sense the presence of her spirit.

On September 30, 2017, my family and I attended a UK game against Eastern Michigan University commemorating the fiftieth anniversary of the desegregation of SEC football. The day before the game, I was interviewed for a documentary titled *Breaking the Barrier*, which was set to air nationally on the SEC Network. A player on the UK football team portrayed me in the on-field reenactment. He wore a helmet and uniform reminiscent of those used in the 1960s when I played. I was told one of my former teammates owned the helmet and had allowed them to use it. The documentary shows a close-up of me looking out at the crowd before running onto the field. At the film's crowning point, the UK player portraying me walks off the field, and as he approaches the goal post in uniform, our images are transposed. I take his place, in my regular clothing. Sort of like the scene in *Field of Dreams*. The scene is very moving.

My original football photo was printed on all the tickets for that game. Posters advertising the game also included my photo, along with two current UK players. Under the photo were the words "50th Anniversary of Nate Northington Integrating SEC Football." During halftime, I went down onto the field, where I received recognition from the fans in attendance and a plaque from the mayor of Lexington proclaiming September 30, 2017, to be Nate Northington Day. Along with that recognition, I was given the keys to the city of Lexington. Finally, a group of over fifty students came onto the field, each wearing a football T-shirt with the number 23 on the front and back. *Wow*, what an honor! And I would learn later that every football player of UK team that day had the number 23 on the back of his helmet and wore my number 23 T-shirt under his uniform during the game. Later I would learn that UK's women's volleyball team wore number 23 in their game against Mississippi State that day in Starkville, Mississippi. I was happy to learn that September 30, 2017, was Nate Northington Day even in the state of Mississippi.

Finally, after the game and UK's victory, I was invited to the locker room to meet the team and coaches and celebrate with the team. To my surprise, I was given the game ball and asked to lead the team in a victory cheer. That really made my day. Regardless of how many games you have played in and how many victories you'll be involved in, there is something special about celebrating another win with the team. This was the icing on the cake.

My wife, children, grandchildren, nephew, and nieces were excited and thrilled by the awesome events and love we received. This was their first time attending a UK football game, so they were completely overjoyed. The game was being filmed for the series. However, they had also never been to a live game on *Saturdays in the South*, so this was an awesome event for them. Being in an SEC football stadium with sixty thousand Big Blue fans cheering and shouting is something they will never forget. They were overwhelmed by the appreciation shown to us and the pageantry taking place. I was grateful that the university was recognizing its history that day.

That same year, I received an SEC Legends Award and was among six recipients of the Michael L. Slive Distinguished Service Award. The other five were Godfrey Dillard, Vanderbilt; Wilbur Hackett, Kentucky; Houston Hogg, Kentucky; Greg Page (posthumous), Kentucky; and Perry Wallace, Vanderbilt.

The master of ceremonies introduced everyone on the dais who would be receiving an award, and when I was introduced as the first African American to play football in the SEC, I received a standing ovation. I was truly moved by the acknowledgment. So when the time came for the Legends Award, the master of ceremonies said, "I don't know about you, but I think we should have the acknowledgment given by the one who had the standing ovation." Another ovation was given, and once again I was touched by the reception. Unfortunately, Perry Wallace, the first African American basketball player in the SEC, died on the day of the dinner. Commissioner Michael L. Slive passed away the next year.

In February 2019, another documentary, titled *Black in Blue*, was produced by a group of former UK players and alumni. This documentary was shown on Kentucky Educational Television and at several locations, including the Worsham Cinema at the UK Gatton Student Center. Once again, I was blessed to see the story of the integration of SEC football being shared with an even broader audience.

A few months later, Karl Schmitt, president of the Louisville Sports Commission, called to inform me that I had been selected for induction into the Kentucky Sports Hall of Fame. The KSHOF includes many great athletes, coaches, and media persons of great distinction. The KSHOF was founded in 1963 to recognize Kentucky natives who have participated in or made a significant impact on their sports in Kentucky. To be chosen for my contributions to sports in my home state, and especially to be included among so many great representatives, was extremely rewarding.

A total of six individuals, including me, were selected for induction in the 2019 class. The others were Derek Anderson, UK and NBA basketball player; Deion Branch, University of Louisville and NFL football standout; William Exum, University of Wisconsin athlete and trailblazer and Kentucky State University administrator; Ralph Hacker, television and radio personality for UK athletics; and Willis Augustus Lee, US Navy rifle team.

All I could say was "Thank you, Jesus!"

Still, the most endearing recognition was the erection of four statues outside Commonwealth Stadium honoring me, Greg Page, Wilbur Hackett, and Houston Hogg. I remember making an invitation list consisting of my family and friends. I have been blessed to have a loving and supporting family along with a lifetime of friends. But how do you make a list of all the people who have supported you and prayed for you throughout a life of almost seventy years? Composing the list reminded me of how truly blessed I had been in my life. My final list, which I did not complete until a few days before the ceremony, totaled forty-nine, and they came from as far away as Boston, Massachusetts. There was a private reception, a press conference, and a private dinner before the official unveiling of the statue.

It was a beautiful day, with excellent weather and plenty of anticipation. When we arrived at the entrance to the stadium, the statues, right in front of the football training complex, were still covered. I was amazed at the sheer size of the covering and couldn't wait to see them. I felt like a child again, ready to unwrap my Christmas presents. But we would have to wait at least two and a half more hours, until after the other events had taken place. As the crowd gathered, including all the news media and dignitaries, I felt so special and so grateful that our legacy in the fight for racial justice will serve as a role model for other generations.

As I was preparing this second edition of *Still Running*, our nation and especially my hometown, Louisville, Kentucky, was gripped by the COVID-19 pandemic. But 2020 also marked the resurgence of mostly nonviolent demonstrations for racial justice and equity. Black men and women had died at the hands of police officers. In March, Breonna Taylor, a Louisville resident, was shot and killed by officers while innocently sleeping in her own apartment as they attempted to serve a no-knock warrant for a drug arrest. The protests surrounding her death and others shed light on the continued presence of racial inequality in America. Health disparities, housing and employment discrimination, and the need for voting rights protection laws remain signature issues in the Black community.

Colin Kaepernick, an African American quarterback with the San Francisco 49ers, had expressed his concern with police violence by taking a knee during the playing of the national anthem at football games a few years earlier. To highlight this ongoing movement, CBS showed the *Forward Progress* documentary again on September 6, 2020, as part of their special titled *Portraits in Black*, a five-part series focusing on the stories of Black athletes who exhibited courage in the face of injustice. In addition to my story were those of tennis greats Arthur Ashe and Althea Gibson, the fourteen Black football players at the University of Wyoming in 1969, and race car driver Bubba Wallace. I appreciated being included in the conversation on racial injustice and felt especially proud of how our accomplishments in 1967 have contributed to our fight for racial justice in our country today.

As I reflected on my own life's journey, I admired the fortitude and courage of all of those persons taking a stand for democracy and racial justice. I was especially proud of the UK athletes, coaches, and administrators who used their platform to support the racial justice movement. I hope and pray that none of them surrender the fight for racial justice.

As a nation, we have come "a mighty long way" since the 1960s. I never dreamed UK would hire Orlando "Tubby" Smith, a Black man, to be the head basketball coach. I never dreamed the SEC would be dominated by Black football players or honor the forerunners like me. And I never dreamed I would have a statue recognizing me as the first Black player in the league. Although Greg Page, my dear friend and brother, did not live to experience all of this with me, he remains in my heart. This book is as much about him as it is about me.

Statue Dedication Speech

Good evening, everyone. This is indeed a tremendous honor and privilege to be here tonight to say a few words on behalf of myself along with my fellow honorees, Greg Page, Wilbur Hackett Jr., and Houston Hogg.

First and foremost, let me give honor to the Lord Jesus Christ, the one who made this event possible. If it were not for his grace and mercy, none of us would be here today.

Also let me give honor to UK president Eli Capilouto and athletics director Mitch Barnhart. I want to commend them for commissioning this monument to honor the four trailblazers of the SEC.

I want to honor all of our parents—the Pages, the Hacketts, the Hoggs, and my parents, the Northingtons. Some are not with us tonight, including my parents, having gone on to eternal life after death, but we are blessed to have some that are still here to celebrate with us on this wonderful occasion. Thank God for all our parents, whose love, support, and guidance enabled us to develop not only into excellent athletes but also into young men of good character and stature. Thank God for our parents. I know they would certainly be proud of us today.

I also want to thank all our siblings and family and friends who supported us and are here today, including my wife and children, my two sisters, one of my brothers, and my niece and nephew.

Thanks to all our teammates, coaches, and administrators. Integrating the University of Kentucky and Southeast Conference football was a complete team effort. There are many people who played a role in this accomplishment: Governor Edward T. Breathitt, the UK Athletics Department, the UK trustees, athletics director Bernie Shively, football coach Charlie Bradshaw, and all the great Big Blue Nation fan base. We could not have done this without the total support of so many at every level.

I want to give special thanks to my former teammates who worked tirelessly and selflessly to ensure my fellow trailblazers, the University of Kentucky, and all supporters receive the credit they deserve from this institution and this state for their role in the integration of the SEC. With fear of leaving out someone, I would be remiss if I did not mention a few of our teammates who played a special part in leading the charge for memorializing us with this statue—like Paul Karem, the late Phil Thompson, Jeff Van Note, Cary Shahid, and Roger Cloyd, just to name a few. Please forgive me for all that I neglected to mention. It was not intentional.

This monument was not without cost. I want to recognize and thank everyone who contributed financially and in any way for your support. You are a part of the team. You are the Big Blue Nation. Thank you!

We should be proud of breaking down the color barrier in the last major conference in the country. I thank God for giving me and my fellow honorees the opportunity to play a role in making history by integrating athletics at UK and in the SEC. Everyone in the Big Blue Nation should be proud of that. This was accomplished during the height of the civil rights movement. We are on the right side of history, and we should be proud of that.

We are proud of the role UK played in supporting us to "change the face of football in the SEC." The University of Kentucky played a historic role in making the SEC the most dominant and most financially successful athletic conference in America today.

This journey was not without difficulty and tragedy. We must always remember the tremendous price Greg Page and his family paid to make this possible. We all paid a price as well. We can't understand the hand of fate or why God allows some traumatic things to happen in our lives, but we know that in his wisdom he is working everything out for a purpose. I am reminded of the scripture that says, "And we know that all things work together for good to them that love God, to them who are the called according to his purpose" (Romans 8:28 KJV). The journey through life is bigger than all of us, but God gives us the grace we need. I am grateful the Lord used us as an agent of change in this country.

Today, because of the contribution we made, Saturdays in Alabama, Mississippi, Georgia, Florida, Tennessee, South Carolina, Missouri, Texas, and Kentucky are the most integrated days of the football season, as people of all colors, races, creeds, religions, and ethnicities come together to support and cheer for their home university. By us integrating the SEC, University of Kentucky football helped change the culture in the South and in America. And it all started right here in the Commonwealth. We should be proud.

I am grateful that Greg Page and I started the change, and I'm thankful that Wilbur and Houston Hogg continued it for us, along with all those who supported us. It was a team effort.

It made me proud that my brother Kenneth Northington followed in my footsteps and played football and ran track at UK. I am also proud that many other African American football players from my high school, Thomas Jefferson, followed in my footsteps to play for the Big Blue. Ken had an opportunity to play on the 1976 Peach Bowl championship team. In just nine short years after integrating the SEC, UK was an SEC and bowl championship team. With the addition of African American athletes like SEC record holder Jim Green in track in 1967, UK became a powerhouse in many other sports.

In conclusion, I am thankful and I am happy that the dream Greg Page had of other Black players following us to play football at UK has come to fruition.

And when we look at the SEC teams play today, with a majority of African American players and the tremendous success it has as the dominant conference in America, it makes me very proud. When we first came to the university and when we walked onto the football field fifty years ago and put on the blue-and-white uniform, we never could have imagined we would be standing here today for such an occasion. And Greg is with us in spirit.

So, on behalf of Greg, Wilbur, Houston, and myself, we say thank you to everyone who came here today to give us this tremendous honor. We are eternally grateful.

May God bless you all!

Fiftieth Anniversary: Nate Northington Day

Being a part of this made me feel special and realize that integration had come a long way, and the efforts and sacrifice we made fifty years ago were well worth it. My only regret is that Greg Page was not there to see the results of our sacrifice. I know he would be smiling and telling me, "Nat, look at what we did." The thought of that makes me smile and say, "Thank you, Lord." I give God all the glory!

SEC Legends and Inaugural SEC Commissioner Michael L. Slive Distinguished Service Award

In July 2017, during the SEC's annual media gathering, SEC commissioner Greg Sankey talked about the integration of sports in the league and the upcoming fiftieth anniversary of that moment. USA Today Network reporter Adam Sparks wrote, "Sankey talked at length . . . about Nate Northington's debut on September 30, 1967, for Kentucky against Mississippi." Sankey said that by playing in a football game "Nate Northington affected all of us." Sankey spoke about the bronze statue erected of all four players and said that the three living players and Greg Page's family had been invited to the league championship game "to join us in remembering, honoring and celebrating what they helped change 50 years ago." Sankey thanked all those who had helped make change happen in the past and those who would help bring change in the future.

I actually saw the article in the *Louisville Courier-Journal* before I received an official invitation to the SEC championship game. I was excited about the article and couldn't wait to get the invitation and take part in the fiftieth anniversary celebration. I couldn't help being full of pride and gratitude. We had come a long way from 1967. It had been a long journey, and finally we were receiving our reward.

I was proud once again to be able to attend the 2017 SEC championship weekend, along with my wife, children, and grandchildren and some of my cousins and church members. This was a jam-packed weekend; in addition to the annual SEC championship game, it also included the SEC Football Legends Dinner, a visit to the College Football Hall of Fame, and filming sessions with the SEC Network for the *Breaking the Barrier* documentary.

The 2017 SEC Legends Dinner took place in Atlanta, Georgia, on December 1, 2017. According to the SEC, the purpose of the SEC Legends Award is "to honor individuals from each SEC League Institution annually whose accomplishments on and off the field have brought pride and distinction to their respective institutions and to the conference." Those honored in this class included Coach Gene Stallings, Alabama; Dan Hampton, Arkansas; Carlos Rogers, Auburn; Danny Wuerffel, Florida; Champ Bailey, Georgia; Glenn Dorsey, Louisiana State; Terrence Metcalf, Mississippi; Floyd Womack, Mississippi State; Brad Smith, Missouri; John Abraham, South Carolina; Chad Clifton, Tennessee; Dave Elmendorf, Texas A&M; Don Orr, Vanderbilt; and me, Nate Northington, Kentucky.

The SEC also honored six individuals who influenced college athletics and the SEC with the Michael L. Slive Distinguished Service Award.

SEC Legends Acknowledgment Speech

Good evening everyone. It is indeed a tremendous honor and privilege to be here tonight and especially to be chosen to give a few remarks on behalf of my fellow honorees. Any one of these great athletes and coaches could have been selected to give these (acknowledgment) remarks, so I am humbled, and I salute each of them.

First and foremost, let's give honor to the Lord Jesus Christ, the one who made this event possible. If it was not for his grace and his mercy, none of us would be here tonight. We certainly take that for granted. For some unknown reason, God has blessed each of us and allowed us to be here on this day and receive this great award. We are indeed thankful.

Then, I would like to give honor to SEC Commissioner Greg Sankey, his staff, and the administrators of the SEC for making such a memorable occasion. They have done an amazing job. Thank you all.

Also, I want to honor all the university presidents, athletics directors, and football coaches at the fourteen SEC institutions who played a role in selecting each of us to represent our respective in the 2017 Legends Class. Each one of us is grateful to receive this prestigious award.

We have been blessed and favored with the love for the game of football, and God gifted us with the talent and work ethic to reach our potential and be able to play this sport at a high level. In addition to equipping us with the attributes to play the game, he blessed us with the people in our lives who supported and encouraged us in the pursuit of our goals and aspirations. This included our parents, siblings, grandparents, aunts and uncles, and many others.

Although my parents are not here tonight, having been called home, I am honored to have my wife and children and some of my grandchildren here tonight, along with some of my friends. I am happy they have the opportunity to be here to support me. I want to thank all of you for without you, I would not be here today. Thank you.

As a child growing up in Louisville, Kentucky, I admired such heroes as heavyweight boxing champion Muhammad Ali and Hall of Fame Basketball player Wes Unseld, and I had great aspirations of being a great athlete one day as well, but I never could have dreamed I would be standing here today receiving this honor.

As a Black person growing up in the South, I have witnessed discrimination on a firsthand basis. I felt God would use me one day to make a difference in this world, and I am grateful he used me to break the color barrier in football in the SEC. When given the opportunity by the Kentucky Governor to accept a football scholarship at the University of Kentucky to become the first African American athlete in the SEC, I felt it was my God-ordained duty and responsibility to accept the calling God had for me, to help bring a change in the greatest football conference in America, and to help change the culture in the country. It was not only me, but Greg Page, my friend and teammate, was also instrumental in this effort by also accepting a scholarship to play in the SEC. Thank you, Greg!

Finally, as has been previously stated, all of the 2017 SEC Legends Class are a highly talented, exceptionally gifted, and incomparable group of football players and coaches, and for me to be included in this group of All-SEC, All-American, All-Pro, Heisman Trophy Winner, and Hall of Fame players and coaches in the greatest football conference in the country, all I can say is WOW! Thank you God!

And thank you all, and God bless you!

1

Yes, Governor

Ask any group of Americans who are nonsoutherners what comes to mind when they think of the South, and you will most likely hear some similar answers. The responses will probably include religion, fried chicken, sweet tea, country music, and racism, and not necessarily in that order. If you ask a sports fan, especially one from Kentucky, the SEC and college sports will definitely be on that list, and probably twice! At the time of this writing, the SEC includes the universities of Florida, Georgia, Kentucky, South Carolina, Tennessee, Vanderbilt, Alabama, Arkansas, Auburn, Louisiana State, Mississippi State, Missouri, Texas A&M, and Mississippi (Ole Miss). When I played in 1967, Arkansas, South Carolina, Missouri, and Texas A&M were not in the league. Arkansas and South Carolina were added in 1991, and Missouri and Texas A&M joined them in 2012.

Many people are surprised to find out that Kentucky, along with the rest of the South, has always been home to some of the best athletes in the world. Of course, nobody is surprised to learn that American sports— certainly in the southern arena—have not always welcomed African Americans.

Even though the US Supreme Court mandated the integration of public schools in the *Brown v. the Board of Education* case of 1954, the South remained defiant. In 1956, the state of Louisiana even passed a law banning its schools from competing in interracial sports. Three years later, in 1959, the US Supreme Court overturned that law.

Mississippi State skipped the NCAA Tournament in 1959, 1961, and 1962 after some of its lawmakers threatened to stop funding schools that competed against integrated teams. In an article titled "Ground Breakers," in the November 7, 2005, edition of *Sports Illustrated*, writer Alexander Wolff commented, "Long after Jackie Robinson smashed the color barrier in baseball, these southern college football pioneers desegregated a more violent sport, in a more violent place, at a more violent time." In the article, Wolff acknowledged the courage it took for these men to integrate the remaining major college football conferences in the South. The men he credited with these achievements included Jerry LeVias of Southern Methodist University in the Southwest Conference, Darryl Hill of Maryland in the Atlantic Coast Conference, and Greg Page, Wilbur Hackett, Houston Hogg, and me of Kentucky in the Southeastern Conference.

The US government sent federal troops to the University of Mississippi in 1962, the year its football team went 10–0. James Meredith was trying to integrate Ole Miss at the time, and the troops there to keep the peace could not prevent riots from breaking out throughout the campus. Meredith succeeded in integrating the university. A documentary titled *Ghosts of Ole Miss* appeared on ESPN Films' *30 for 30* series in recognition of the fiftieth anniversary of these events. The article noted that white southerners did not approve of integrating their football teams any more than they did their classrooms.

This happened so long ago, and today it seems strange because Black athletes are the dominant performers in the once all-white SEC. In today's SEC, African American players easily constitute between 65 and 70 percent of the football rosters.

By all appearances, the racial tension did not seem as strong at the University of Kentucky (UK), where in May 1963 the school's athletics board declared that it wanted all UK sports teams integrated "as soon as possible." Nevertheless, after he became university president in 1963, John Oswald found that, in spite of their efforts, legendary basketball coach Adolph Rupp and football coach Charlie Bradshaw had not succeeded in signing Black athletes to integrate their teams. Oswald was born in Minnesota and educated in California, so he was a proponent of desegregation. In his column for the newspaper the *Cats' Pause*, longtime contributor Russell Rice wrote, "Oswald let it be known that he expected all coaches to recruit Black players and that UK could lose a large amount of federal funding if they did not do so." He created a Student Affairs Department with the goal of integrating sports, but that did not immediately succeed.

Rice, who worked for the UK Athletics Department for two decades, indicates that although Florida, Tennessee, and Vanderbilt expressed a desire to integrate their athletic teams, they felt that Kentucky should be the first to make the move because it was the northernmost state in the conference. But because things were very rough in those days, nothing happened.

Many articles have been written about Coach Rupp's unsuccessful recruitment of Wes Unseld in 1964 and of Butch Beard in 1965. I am not aware of all the facts regarding Unseld, Beard, or other African American recruits, but I am quite certain that one of their main concerns was the reality of traveling to the Deep South during a time of racial turmoil and hostility. There would be no problem playing home games in Lexington, but being a pioneer and traveling to play ball in places where they were not accepted would have been extremely dangerous. Remember, this was the time of the Civil Rights Act of 1964. The law dealt mainly with public accommodations, meaning that Blacks could no longer be excluded from restaurants, hotels, and other public facilities. But passage of the law was one thing; getting the hotels and restaurants to comply was entirely another. It would take sit-ins, marches, court battles, pain, suffering, sacrifice, and a lot of prayer before that would happen. School administrators and coaches knew that finding accommodations for their integrated teams would be extremely difficult and very dangerous. So any universities wanting to integrate their athletic teams would need to overcome serious problems, and traveling in the South during these times would have been monumentally difficult. The job of convincing the players and their families to accept a scholarship was a daunting one at best, and neither Coach Rupp nor Coach Bradshaw succeeded. After signing with the University of Louisville, both Unseld and Beard went on to become college All-Americans and NBA All-Stars. Unseld was also voted into the NBA Hall of Fame.

Since UK missed out on signing Unseld and Beard, the focus of SEC integration efforts turned to the football program. In a *Los Angeles Times* article dated September 3, 2004, staff writer David Wharton reports that Rice claimed that Oswald had made his football coach an unusual offer: if Charlie Bradshaw would recruit Black players, the university would guarantee him employment for life, even if he was fired as coach. Rice writes in the December 15, 2007, article for the *Cats' Pause*, "At the end of that season [1965], the university gave Bradshaw a new contract of indeterminate length. The following month, he broke the Southeastern Conference football color barrier by signing Nat Northington of Louisville to a UK grant." The next month, Greg Page signed to become the second African American in the SEC. *Did* UK make this offer to Bradshaw so he would recruit and sign Black players? I must say I was totally shocked when I first read this article by Rice while I was doing research for this book. I was totally unaware of the offer, and if Greg Page knew about it, he never mentioned anything of this nature to me. I would like to believe that we were both recruited by Bradshaw and UK because of our qualifications as football players and our character. In fact, a *Louisville Courier-Journal* article by Bob Cooper dated February 5, 1967, quotes Bradshaw: "We have a set of criteria that we apply to all the young men we seek, and they must measure up to these standards athletically, academically, and in their personal lives." While he indicated that we met these qualifications, Bradshaw never mentioned any special agreements made between him and Dr. Oswald regarding incentives or conditions for recruiting Black football players. I would like to believe that we were recruited and signed strictly on the basis of our own merits. In all fairness to Bradshaw, he is not here to comment on this story.

So after the UK Athletics Board adopted an official policy in 1963, it took two years for the school to integrate its sports team. The UK student newspaper, the *Kentucky Kernel*, was instrumental in placing a spotlight on the administration, and other news organizations contributed to the effect.

While the Kentucky administration and coaching staff were determining the best ways to integrate the UK and SEC football programs, I was developing into an extremely competitive football player. In 1964, as a junior at Thomas Jefferson High School, I had an outstanding season, leading the Jefferson County Public Schools of Louisville, Kentucky, in touchdowns and scoring, while making the All-County and All-State teams. Then in 1965, I again made the All-State football team, in spite of missing three games because of a broken hand, which cost me any chance of repeating as scoring champion. I was second in scoring behind my teammate Ron Gathright. We had an outstanding team, compiling a 9–1 record and playing for the county championship. We missed an opportunity to play for the AAA State Title by one point—losing the game by a disappointing score of 7–6. A tie would have given us the championship and a shot at the state title.

Academically, I was an honor student, with the fourth-highest grade point average in my senior class. I also served as an officer in the Beta Club and National Honor Society. My parents ensured I made academics and my college education a top priority—higher even than sports. As Coach Bradshaw mentioned in the *Courier-Journal* article, it was important that the school recruit athletes who were good students with excellent character, in addition to being outstanding football players. I am sure UK vetted all this before putting me on its recruiting list.

Back then, players like me who made the All-State teams usually got an invitation to the governor's mansion for a recognition dinner. I made the teams and went to the dinners. This was a great honor, and I was excited, but it was my last visit that I really love to remember. The governor's mansion is a public building and a private residence for the governor and his family. It is open to the public, so for a fee, anybody can visit on a Tuesday or Thursday or request a special appointment to see it, and thousands of people do just that each year. My last trip was special because we didn't have to contact the capitol tour desk or request a special visit; Governor Edward Thompson "Ned" Breathitt Jr. invited us himself! My high school football coach informed my parents of the invitation. Despite what others felt or thought, Dr. John W. Oswald, the UK president at the time, was committed to integrating UK's athletic program. He and the governor showed a true interest in civil rights, and their concern was an instrumental factor in my becoming the first African American football player in the SEC. The *New York Times* wrote in Breathitt's obituary, published on October 16, 2003, that the governor, who served from 1963 to 1967, "made civil rights his theme at a time when few politicians below the Mason-Dixon line would do so."

As a student at Newburg Elementary School, I went on a field trip with my classmates to Frankfort, Kentucky, the state capital. One of the places we visited was the governor's mansion. As a nine- or ten-year-old, I had no earthly way of knowing or expecting that one day my entire family and I would be invited back to have dinner with the governor of the state of Kentucky.

The UK recruiters felt they needed support and a little gubernatorial intervention to sell me on the benefits of playing football at UK. The assistant coach, George Boone, had even gone to my sister Rose's college campus at Catherine Spalding College in downtown Louisville to ask for her help in persuading me to sign. They used some very strong tactics, but at the time, I had not made up my mind and was leaning toward either Purdue University or the University of Louisville. Both schools were heavily recruiting me. Purdue had scouted me since I was a junior in high school, and I knew that the Big Ten Conference had integrated many years earlier and had some outstanding Black All-Americans, such as Sherman Lewis of Michigan State, who is a graduate of Louisville duPont Manual High School. Gene Washington, Bubba Smith, and Clinton Jones are a few other Black All-Americans to have come out of that conference. The University of Louisville was in the Missouri Valley Conference, which had integrated teams as well.

Even though I was still undecided, whenever I was asked where I was going, I responded that I did not think I would go to UK. Remember that UK had not invited Blacks to attend in the past, and given the racial climate during those times, few Blacks were lining up to play football in the Deep South. When you are in the position that I was in, your friends ask many questions about your choices. It is easy to give in to pressure and do what other people want you to do, rather than following your own heart, but I just was not raised that way. My parents were decisive people, and watching my dad over the years taught me to be decisive and to follow my convictions.

Playing football was tough enough without dealing with the kinds of problems one could expect to encounter as a trailblazer. I had heard enough about Jackie Robinson and the trials he faced. Yes, I had followed UK football and basketball on the radio and in the newspapers, and I had accepted an invitation to a football game in Lexington in the fall of 1965, my senior year of high school. Although I was not seriously expecting to attend the university, I felt it was always good to explore any available options and to avoid closing the door on opportunities, so I accepted the invitation issued through my high school coach and went to the game. It was exciting and entertaining, with UK winning a close and hard-fought game. I was impressed with the team, the fans, and the total atmosphere, but I was still leaning toward Purdue or the University of Louisville.

I think I must have said that to the wrong person, because word seemed to have gotten back to the coaches. That was when the big push began. UK was playing hardball to get me to join them. When they hit me with the once-in-a-lifetime personal invitation to the governor's mansion, that was the icing on the cake. Although I did not feel pressured, it is not an easy thing to turn down the governor of the state.

My family accepted the governor's invitation to dinner, and on a Sunday afternoon, December 19, 1965, we packed up the whole family: my mother and father; my two younger brothers, Michael and Kenneth; and my sister Rose. My older brothers, James and William Jr., and my sister Barbara were married at that time and did not accompany us on the trip. We all put on our Sunday best, got into my father's 1961 Chevrolet Bel Air sedan, and drove to Frankfort to have dinner with Governor Breathitt. Dad likes nice cars, and we always had a late-model auto. The drive was only around fifty miles or so, but it seemed to take a week.

The governor's mansion was impressive, and we felt honored to have been invited. Only a handful of executive residences in the United States are open to the public, so you can imagine the joy and surprise that I felt when Governor Breathitt invited us. These days, security is high at the mansion, but back then, they did not search us as they do the visitors who come from around the world every week. Although this was not my first visit, I was still awestruck by the sheer beauty of the stately mansion and the fabulous furnishings. It was only five days until Christmas, so all the trees and decorations were festive. The dining room featured majestic carpeting, bright, comfortable sofas, colorful curtains, a solid-mahogany table, and numerous chairs. It was extremely elegant.

I had forgotten what we had for dinner until my sister reminded me. It was a traditional dinner. We had cold salad and warm rolls, and then came the tender roast beef, fresh vegetables, creamy mashed potatoes, and gravy, as well as a few other trimmings. I guess you would expect a delicious dinner at the governor's mansion.

After dessert, Governor Breathitt invited me, along with my coach, Jim Gray, to his office, which was quite impressive and beautifully decorated with plenty of polished wood trim and an exquisite array of fine furniture. As we sat across from each other in comfortable chairs, he gave me a convincing presentation about going to UK. The governor was a relatively young man who had supported civil rights and the passage of civil rights legislation. Now he sincerely desired that UK integrate its athletic programs. He explained that the time had come and that it was critical that UK lead the way in the integration of the SEC. He told me that the UK Board of Trustees and President John Oswald fully supported integration. He said that I met all the criteria to be the first to integrate UK's athletic program and that I was an outstanding candidate, given my athletic ability, scholastic achievement, and character. I was also a Kentuckian, and that was a critical factor as well.

He talked about the tremendous impact my integrating the SEC would have not only for Blacks but also for whites. I believe the governor was making me aware that we are all interdependent. In other words, every member of our society is mutually dependent on the others. He quoted Dr. Martin Luther King Jr.'s "Letter from Birmingham Jail," written on April 16, 1963, saying that "injustice anywhere is a threat to justice everywhere." In 1965, the entire country was aware of the fight for civil rights for all Americans, especially for African Americans in the South, where Jim Crow laws and practices were common. I believe that history has shown that sports have always had a significant impact in bringing people of different races together. Integrating the athletic programs in the SEC would remove one of the last vestiges of segregation in the South and move the country forward. I have to admit that the pressure was really on at that point. The governor spoke about the many benefits of staying in Kentucky to play ball, such as being close to my family and friends, since Louisville was fewer than seventy-five miles from Lexington. At that point, I even remembered that Dad loved to come to all my games. The governor also mentioned that playing at home would be a factor in my professional career and that it would expose me to greater options once my football career was over. He was a good salesman, really good, but I held to my principles of making my own decisions—that is, until he mentioned that little issue of being the first African American to "break the color barrier" in the SEC.

After he spoke of the tremendous significance of this event and the everlasting impact it would have, not only on me but on other African

American athletes throughout the South, he pulled a scholarship offer from his coat pocket and asked if I would agree to accept and play football for my home state. At that point, not only was I convinced but I thought it was the right thing to do. These may not be my exact words, but I looked him straight in the eye, shook his hand, and said, "Governor Breathitt, I accept this scholarship."

There was no way I could have ever imagined the kind of impact this would have on my life and the lives of my family members. Once I agreed to accept the scholarship, everything went into high speed for the next twenty-four hours. Somebody must have immediately notified the media, because they were Johnny-on-the-spot! We got in the governor's limo and headed to Lexington to meet with UK president John Oswald and Coach Charlie Bradshaw for the official signing. In the UK archives is a picture of me signing documents with the governor as Dr. Oswald and others watch. After the photo sessions, we got back in the limo and went to Thomas Jefferson High School in Louisville, where Coach Gray; my high school principal, W. D. Bruce; and more local media met us. When all that was finally completed, the governor's driver took us home in the limo.

An Associated Press story dated December 20, 1965, noted that the governor had "entertained the star football player from Louisville at a luncheon at the Governor's Mansion, then started off on a two-city hop with the athlete" that culminated at my home.

My friends said they looked out their window and saw this long black limo going down my street, and they wondered what was going on. Then they remembered that my family and I had gone to Frankfort to have dinner with the governor, and they knew that must be me coming home in the governor's limo. You see, this was years before instant news flashes that let you see events on television minutes after they happen. They had to come by to get the news firsthand. They were surprised—*shocked* may be a better word—but they supported me 100 percent. They were true friends, and although they wanted me to do something different, they respected my decision.

Even to this day, my friends and I laugh and talk about that cold December day in 1965 when the governor's big smooth limo came bouncing down our bumpy, pothole-laden street.

Of all the experiences that began my college football career, some stand out significantly: the dinner, the mansion, the joy in my mom's and dad's eyes, the feeling in my heart. All these things are pleasantly engraved in my memory. How many eighteen-year-olds who are not on a tour get into the governor's office or sit at that huge state dinner table and then ride down their own bumpy neighborhood street in a private limo? Although I felt "those were the days," that was truly just the beginning.

In an interview for the University of Kentucky Oral History Project in 2000, the governor talked about the time he recruited me:

> Oswald wanted to integrate athletics, as President of the University. He came from California, University of California system. He was recruited during Combs' period as governor and chairman, the year before I became governor . . . so Oswald and I said we were just going to do it. Now the Athletic Director was Bernie Shively, who's from Illinois and played football, was a star at the University of Illinois. They had been integrated. He had played with African-Americans. There wasn't any problem for the Athletic Director. . . . And we recruited Nate Northington from Louisville to come to U. K. We had him and his whole family over to the Governor's mansion after church for a late Sunday dinner. And Oswald and I talked to him, and we told him we would get him another African-American. And we recruited one, and to our distress he was killed in practice.
>
> So this Nate had to then survive as the only one there. They were roommates. And we pointed out to him what it would mean. He would integrate the whole Southeastern Conference. There was not an African-American on scholarship or playing on any team in the Southeastern Conference. And this was years after we had integrated the University. But athletics was not integrated.

I did not have the opportunity to meet Governor Breathitt again until twenty-eight years later in 1993, when I accepted an invitation to a UK Board of Trustees meeting to be recognized and to receive a plaque for my accomplishments. UK summoned me to honor me as the first African American to sign a letter of intent and play football in the SEC. That was all fine and well, but technically speaking, even though I was the first to play, my roommate, Greg Page, and I both arrived at UK in the same year. I'm sure they had already planned to recognize him, but I told them I would go only if they also gave a plaque to Greg Page's family. They agreed, and I went. I will always remember Greg Page and will do all I can to ensure others do so as well.

After all the excitement of that first meeting with the governor and the whirlwind of events, it was time to get back to school and back to normal, or so I thought. I was sure the celebration would be over, but it was actually just beginning. There was nothing normal about that Monday.

I was the talk of the school. My principal had been part of the signing ceremony at the school that Sunday night, and now it was time for all the teachers and my classmates to take part in this historic event. They were not quite ready for me to start signing my autograph, but they congratulated me, letting me know how proud they were of me and how glad they were that I was part of their lives as a member of Thomas Jefferson High School and as their friend.

I believe they were more excited than I was, but I guess I have always been sort of low-key about things. Many of the teachers and students were obviously UK fans, and several teachers were UK graduates, so I felt very good about my decision and about having such great support. I was proud and happy to have so many good friends as classmates and teachers.

Stories appeared in newspapers and other media for days after my signing. Someone even sent me a newspaper article from the December 20, 1965, edition of the *New York Journal-American* that had a photo showing me with my mom and sister Rose, the governor, the principal, my high school coach, and the UK coaches. The caption said I was "to become the first Negro to sign a Southeastern Conference athletic grant-in-aid." After I received that, it really drove home the magnitude of what had just happened.

The *New York Times* also reported on December 20, 1965, under the headline "Kentucky Gives Scholarship to Negro Athlete First Time": "For the first time the University of Kentucky has given an athletic grant-in-aid to a Negro. He is Nat Northington, a star back and an 'A' student."

Dr. Oswald expressed satisfaction and relief that the university had successfully signed a Black athlete to a scholarship, after unsuccessful attempts to recruit Black athletes in the past. Again, I only became aware of this article while writing my story, and I am sure that many other articles in newspapers, magazines, and other media sources throughout the country reported this historic event. I recall seeing articles about it in *Jet* and *Ebony*.

So how did an extraordinarily athletic, intelligent, unassuming, shy teenager raised in the little community of Newburg come to be honored in such a way? Well, that goes all the way back to my birth in the significant year of 1947, in a historic and remarkable little community known by the name of Little Africa.

2

Little Africa

There's a popular old one-liner that goes, "I was born in '47, but I was too young to remember." That's only funny because it's already understood that normal people don't remember events that occur at birth. In general, I know that my childhood was a happy one, and as an athlete, I believe the year of my birth is significant. It was the year that a civil rights committee under President Harry Truman officially condemned racial injustices toward African Americans. Dr. Martin Luther King Jr., who was eighteen years old at the time, delivered his first sermon at Ebenezer Baptist, his father's church in Atlanta. A year prior, race riots had erupted in places like Philadelphia and Athens, Alabama. All across America and in Louisville, good things were happening for Black folk, and some not-so-good things were happening to Black folk. Fortunately, none of the negative things kept me from my destiny. I believe certain things happen for a reason. I also believe God prepares the way for whatever mission he has for your life.

The Bible says, in the book of Psalms, "The steps of a good man are ordered by the Lord: and he delighteth in his way" (Psalm 37:23 KJV). If you study this passage in the original Hebrew, you will see that the word *good* was supplied by the translators. It is not part of the original text. In other words, God orders the steps of a man (the man God chooses for a task). The late bishop Norman Wagner once said, "When God gives vision, he also gives provision." In other words, God will make a way for his plan and his man to accomplish the mission that he has appointed and ordained.

When I was a young Black male, the negatives of the 1940s were the devil's design to defeat me, but God ordered the positives to promote me. On April 15, 1947, Jack Roosevelt "Jackie" Robinson became the first African American to play Major League Baseball. He broke the so-called color barrier in the major leagues. From that point forward, God set things into motion that would pave the way for the sports path I would follow. You see, I believe my birth the same year as this historical event was not just a coincidence. I believe that it was all ordained by God and that he would lead, direct, and prepare me for my destiny in life. In a later chapter, I will expound on other facts about Jackie Robinson's life that will shed more light on why I feel the way I do.

I imagine that in 1947 life was easier for children than it is today. Back then, many American children were happy to simply run, jump, and play with toys as simple as pogo sticks, baseballs, and footballs. Television was just catching on. People listened primarily to radio—AM radio at that. It must have felt good to gather around and hear a baseball game on the radio.

In 1947, the average pay per year was approximately $2,850. A new house at that time probably cost around $6,000 or so. For a struggling family, however, $6,000 may have seemed like $6 million. Even with the low prices of gasoline (fifteen cents a gallon) and a loaf of bread (thirteen cents), adults of that decade still struggled to make ends meet. Think about it. If you didn't have a car, why would you care about the low cost of gas?

I don't know exactly what struggles my parents were dealing with when I was born, but if you factor in race, it seems clear they would have had their plates full just trying to make it. To the world, I was nobody special, but God performed his own version of alchemy. That is what God does in the life of his people. Alchemy is taking something ordinary and turning it into something extraordinary, often in a way that cannot be explained.

I think that, by the grace of God, I was blessed. Although I had to go through trials and tribulations as a young Black boy in the 1950s and 1960s, I believe God had his hand of protection on me. In spite of all that was going on, he enabled me to simply fall in love with sports and focus on it while I was growing up.

I was the third son and fifth child of William E. and Flossie Northington. The birth took place at home, as was the norm at the time, especially for poor folk. We lived at Thirty-Second Street and Magnolia Avenue next door to my paternal grandparents, Norman and Lucy Northington, deep in Louisville's West End. I say *deep* because it was about as far west as you could go before arriving at the Ohio River.

In the years that followed my arrival, my mother gave birth to two more sons. My brothers are James, William Edward Jr., Michael, and Kenneth. I also have two older sisters, Barbara Jean and Rose Marie. Barbara is the oldest, followed by James, William Jr., Rose, me, Michael, and Kenneth. God blessed us with reasonably good health, for which we are grateful. One other son, who would have been the baby, was born to my parents, but he died shortly after birth. My parents brought me into this world the same year Henry Ford died. It was also the same year Tupperware was invented. I am a baby boomer.

Mom and Dad grew up during a time when the majority of Black folk were not able to get very much formal education, but they were always very industrious and extremely hardworking. They met when Mom's family moved to Dad's neighborhood when she was a young teenager. Dad said she was the prettiest of her five sisters and had long black hair. I believe he was lovestruck. During a time when African Americans really struggled to find decent employment and pay, my parents were able to raise seven children while working hard at manual labor. They succeeded in professions that required strict punctuality, loyalty, and the willingness to pay attention to detail. Back then, it really didn't matter what color you were. If you wanted to keep your job, you needed to have good qualities like Mom and Dad had.

My father's parents moved to Louisville from Hopkinsville, Kentucky, before he was born. My father was the oldest boy in his family. However, he had a twin brother who died at birth. He had four sisters and two other brothers. As with most young boys in those days, as the oldest son, Dad had to give up formal schooling at an early age, as a teenager, to help support his family. He didn't have much formal education, but thanks to mother wit, Dad was able to manage quite nicely. Mother wit is what helped Harriet Tubman lead Black people to freedom. It helped the freed slaves survive, stay safe, and keep their newfound freedom. Mother wit is about knowing when and when not to talk. It is a folksy kind of wisdom that helps people make it through tough times and achieve their goals even when life seems impossible. Mother wit is a real quality, and I am convinced my father had it. He was a crafty, intelligent man who possessed more than a wealth of good old common sense.

My parents were not complainers. They were fighters, especially Dad, who dabbled in amateur boxing when he was younger. He was also a fighter in the sense that he was not a quitter. Dad was always determined to accomplish whatever he set his mind to.

My father was an industrious man. He loved and protected his family and would stop at nothing to improve our quality of life. His main profession was concrete finishing, but he was also a brick mason and a carpenter. He worked on many of the high-rise buildings and parking garages in downtown Louisville, pouring concrete foundations and floors. He also worked on many homes and streets in the new subdivisions in Louisville. My father built every house we owned. That itself was truly a remarkable achievement for a southern Black man in the 1940s, '50s, and '60s.

Dad took me to work with him when he was doing a job for someone in the neighborhood. I helped mix mortar, carry blocks and bricks, dig footers, and other manual labor. I am sure the various jobs I performed with Dad—and the chores I was required to do at home—contributed to my character and helped me develop the physical strength, stamina, and work ethic I needed to become an outstanding athlete and man of conviction.

Our pastor would use Dad's talents on various building projects for our church. My father was a man of great character and was well respected in the community. He would treat other people with respect and would do just about anything for anyone. If there was ever a man who believed in working hard, it was my dad, and he taught us the same work ethic.

Who could forget the love and support that they received from a dad like mine? He supported all his children in every way he could. Whenever there was a game, I knew he would be there the whole time, walking up and down the sidelines. I couldn't see him all the time, but when I did catch a glimpse of him, he was as excited as he was when we would watch Jim Brown run for the Cleveland Browns on Sunday afternoons.

I believe the last game Dad saw me play was at Western Kentucky. He was so proud of our accomplishments. Even after all these years, when I am watching certain games, Dad occasionally comes to mind. I think of the ways he reacted to the plays, the things he said, and the lessons he taught us. Above all, no matter what was happening in my life, I could always count on my father. Dad passed away in October 2008 at age eighty-eight, but his memory will always be with me. My wife, Gwendolyn, says that as long as I live, she will never forget Dad because many of my actions remind her of him. He could sometimes be a real jokester, and he loved to make everyone laugh. He always taught us to treat everyone the way we wanted to be treated.

Mom was born in Mississippi and moved to Louisville at age fourteen with her family. She was a domestic worker, employed in the home of a prominent attorney and his music-teacher wife. Not only did Mom raise her own children well but she also worked very hard at helping raise that attorney's three children. Mom's employers so appreciated her that they made sure Social Security funds were paid into her account so she would receive benefits when she retired, something few people who employed domestic workers did.

When mom's employers celebrated their fiftieth wedding anniversary, they made sure my mother received an invitation—not as a worker but as a friend. The generosity and respect they had for my mother were due in part to the great character and love she exhibited. Gestures like that were almost unheard of back in those times.

My mother would go without things for herself so we could have the things we needed, and many times even the things we merely wanted. When I was about thirteen years old, I saw a nice baseball glove in a newspaper ad. That glove was the hottest thing going at the time. I wanted it really badly and told my mother about it. My eyes lit up like Christmas bulbs when she said she would get it for me. It took a few weeks, but she saved and saved until she had enough to buy me that glove. As you can imagine, that meant an awful lot to me. I can never forget the sacrifices my mother made for me. That's the kind of mother she was. If she could do anything for her children, she would, and she didn't complain or make you feel sorry for asking.

Mom was also a tremendous advocate for education. She was intelligent and as knowledgeable as most college graduates. She was determined to make sure we got as much education as we could. She was an avid reader who kept abreast of current events and world affairs. She knew the value and power of a college education. She instilled in us the need for college, and she encouraged us in every way she could. With Mom, there was no such thing as not doing your best in school. She was capable of helping with our homework, and she made sure we got it done. More important than anything else, my mother was a great spiritual inspiration to my siblings and me. She loved the Lord with all her heart, and she was an example not only to her own family but also to the entire community.

Mom was one of those people who, when you saw her, you knew loved the Lord even before she opened her mouth. If ever there was an example of a witness to a family or community, Mom was it. Mom was a quiet person, but she lived the life of a saint of God and let her actions serve as a witness. Mom's faith and passion caused the people around her to accept Jesus into their hearts and minds. She is the reason all my siblings are baptized in Jesus's name.

She was a gifted spiritual singer, and for many years she sang "He Was There All the Time." I thank God that, throughout my entire life, Mom was there for me all the time, and in many ways, she still is. I have always been proud of my mother.

Mom and Dad were married for sixty-seven years when Dad passed, and I could always tell they loved each other very much. Thanks to them, I still look back and consider my childhood among the best times of my life. I can honestly say I am proud to be a product of my parents.

I am blessed to have grown up knowing all my grandparents and to have had the opportunity to spend some considerable time around all of them. My paternal grandfather would work on his job from sunup until sundown and was kind and loving to all his children and grandchildren. Some of my fondest memories of Granddaddy Norman Northington are of this little, short man, with several of his grandchildren tagging along, walking a few blocks to the store, where he would buy them candy and other goodies. On the Fourth of July, he would travel several miles in the wee hours of the morning to hold a spot for all the family to celebrate at Chickasaw Park. All my uncles, aunts, and cousins would meet there, along with thousands of other Blacks, to spend the day. We would always get new clothes and shoes. At the park, we would eat the delicious food prepared by

my southern-bred aunts and grandparents. Those were great times. I thank
God that as I was growing up my life and family were rich with positive
role models, especially my parents and grandparents.

One of the cousins we played with, Albert Northington, made history
by becoming the first African American basketball coach to win the girls'
Kentucky State Basketball Championship.

Way, way back in the history of Kentucky, people called the area we
lived in "the Homestead." At one time in segregated Louisville, folks called
this same area "Needmore" or "Little Africa." Just as the name suggests,
Little Africa was the Black section of what is now Parkland. I have to admit
that while growing up I did not realize the significance of this community.
Today, however, when I look back, I realize the kind of pride and fortitude
my parents, my grandparents, and all those in my community embodied.
The majority of my uncles, aunts, and cousins lived in Little Africa, and
they shared a community bond that went beyond being members of the
same family.

Louisville is the largest city in Kentucky, but when African Americans
wanted to own a business back in the day, Little Africa was one of the few
places they could.

There is a historical marker for Little Africa about two blocks from my
former home on Grand Avenue (the same street Muhammad Ali lived on)
and from the former Virginia Avenue Elementary School, where I attended
first and second grade.

The marker reads: "Located west of 32nd and south of Garland Ave.,
'Little Africa' was original African American section of Parkland. Settled in
1870s, African Americans first called it 'Needmore.' 'Little Africa' evolved
from a shantytown into a thriving community by 1920, with several hundred
homes, six churches, and various businesses and schools.

"'Little Africa' embodied the black self-help ethic. The Parkland
Improvement Club helped to add items such as cinder walks and mailbox-
es to the community. The town of 'Little Africa' disappeared ca. 1948 when
work began on the Cotter Homes Project, named for early resident, poet,
and educator Joseph S. Cotter (1861–1949)."

In the 1950s, the Louisville Municipal Housing Commission had a
large portion of the neighborhood demolished to make way for two public

housing complexes, Cotter Homes and Lang Homes. Thanks to a massive revitalization effort bolstered by a $400 million investment in the 1990s, the public housing complexes were developed into a mixed-income development, and Little Africa is once again a thriving community with hundreds of apartments, new homes, stores, health clinics, senior housing, nursing homes, public schools, city parks, and churches. Little Africa is now called Park DuValle and is a national model and award-winning community.

When I was five or six, we moved a few miles to Grand Avenue, where one of our neighbors was none other than Cassius Clay—otherwise known as Muhammad Ali. Clay, who was five years older than me, was one of my boyhood sports idols. We went to the same elementary school as he did, and my sister Barbara was a classmate of Ali's brother, Rudy Clay. Later in life, when I was in my twenties, Ali built a home for his parents in the southeast Louisville neighborhood of Montclair, and once again, it was only a few blocks away from my parents' home. A crowd would gather whenever the word got around that he was in town, and he would come out and entertain all the folks in the neighborhood.

As a child, I would watch Cassius box every week on WAVE-TV, a local NBC-affiliated station. It aired a show called *Tomorrow's Champions*. Many local Louisville fighters, like World Boxing Association champion Jimmy Ellis, appeared on the show. Ellis got into boxing by watching Clay. When I saw Cassius box when he was fourteen or fifteen years old and I was around nine, I predicted he would be great. I have always loved boxing, and I loved to watch young Cassius. He was so fast on his feet and quick with his hands that he would usually overwhelm his opponents with a constant barrage of punches. When Ali won the Olympic gold medal in 1960, droves of well-wishers, the news media, and dignitaries of the city welcomed him home. They even held a grand parade in his honor.

Even though it looked as if everybody loved him, Ali told quite a different story. He said that after all the hoopla died down, he went to a local restaurant one day to eat. Because of racism and the Jim Crow laws that were in place at the time, he was denied the right to sit at the counter. The champ said this hurt him for years—so much so that he stood on the Clark Memorial Bridge in downtown Louisville and threw his gold medal into the Ohio River.

Even though people debate whether this really happened, Ali stuck to his story. He wrote about it in his autobiography, *The Greatest: My Own Story*, written with Richard Durham and published in 1975. Regardless of how he was treated back then, Muhammad Ali was always a great ambassador of peace and justice, both for the city and for America. Today in downtown Louisville, a museum honors his life and boxing legacy. I had the privilege of meeting Muhammad Ali on several occasions, and some of those times I got his autograph and took a few pictures with him.

When he fought for the World Heavyweight Championship in 1964, I was a junior in high school. He was going up against Sonny Liston, and Ali was a huge underdog. Here was our twenty-two-year-old hometown hero with only two years' professional experience taking on this powerful champion, who had destroyed then heavyweight champion Floyd Patterson in two fights, each time in one round, to take and retain the title.

The media "experts" said Liston would destroy Clay as well, but my friends and I knew better. Nine or ten of us met at a friend's house and gathered around the radio to listen to the highlights of the fight. After each round, the announcer gave a summary. We cheered when we heard that Clay had won the round, and we moaned when things were going against him, but that was not often. Ali was simply dazzling as he methodically took Liston apart, hitting him from all angles. Sonny could not get out of the way. Finally, Sonny Liston refused to come out to fight in the seventh round. While sitting in his corner, Liston told his trainers that he had injured his shoulder and could not continue.

When the referee declared Clay the winner, the room erupted in celebration. We jumped up and ran into the streets to celebrate with the rest of our neighborhood. Our hometown hero and Olympic champion was now the heavyweight champion of the world. Words cannot describe the joy and pride we felt. I like to watch the tapes of that match even to this day.

I believe I last saw him in person around 2002, when he came to visit his brother, Rahman Ali, who was also a heavyweight boxer. Rahman, born Rudolph Valentino Clay, lived in the building where I worked for the Louisville Metro Housing Authority, at the corner of Eighth Street and Muhammad Ali Boulevard. Our offices were on the first floor in a high-rise residential building, and the second floor and above are reserved for the residents' apartments.

I remember one day as I was returning from my lunch break, I noticed a large number of fellow employees looking through a glass door that separates our office from the residents' lobby. I asked what was going on, and when I looked through the door, Muhammad Ali was surrounded by employees and residents. I went into the hall, where he was doing one of the things he did best: holding court. Even then, he was visibly suffering from the effects of Parkinson's disease. Still, there he was telling jokes, performing magic tricks, and just being the entertainer he was. He loved magic tricks, and he even demonstrated his ability to levitate. He also did one of the standard magic tricks of making a handkerchief disappear.

Of course, all the women wanted to hug him and give him a kiss—and of course, he accommodated them. They were just going wild.

As I stood beside him, he had just hugged a young woman, a coworker of mine, who had kissed him on the cheek. He leaned over and whispered to me, "I got all the women."

I told him, "You sure do." I understood what he meant by those words. He was jokingly letting me know that as a famous celebrity he attracted the attention of many seeking to capitalize on his fame and fortune and that he had to be on guard at all times.

I compared his speech (which was barely audible) and movements with what they had been when he was heavyweight champ. The difference was striking. Back then, he had spat out jokes and comments nonstop. Now he had someone with him who often spoke for him. This did not diminish his impact on people, and everyone was thrilled to be in his presence. Ali was a thinker, and all his actions had a reason or purpose behind them. Even when he told jokes, they were not idle jokes; they all had a deeper meaning and a message. He was obviously speaking to make you think. He told a number of jokes that day as well, and we were all just rolling in laughter. That was an enjoyable experience and one I will always remember.

3

It Takes a Village

Newburg

When I was eight years old, my father moved us outside the city limits to a rural part of the county. He told us we were moving to a place where we could have farm animals, but I knew my dad. He wanted to get us out of the negative environment of the fast-growing city neighborhoods where we had always lived. Moving always brings mixed emotions, especially for children. I had never read the book of Philippians, but as the move drew closer, I could have used a good dose of Philippians 4:6: "Be anxious for nothing, but in everything by prayer and supplication, with thanksgiving, let your requests be made known to God" (NKJV).

At first we were excited and hoped for the best. We interpreted the move to mean we were going to have a nice big farm. As children, we went along with it because we had to, but we didn't really understand the choice that our industrious father was making. One thing was certain: as the moving date drew closer, our anxiety and our need for that Philippians verse grew.

We didn't panic, but we did have some questions that we asked silently—important questions like "Whom will we play with?" and "Where will we go to school?" We were comfortable in our old home and neighborhood. Why did we need new surroundings? At first it seemed so quiet in the rural area that we wondered where all the people were and whether they had any kids out there. Soon the reality of missing our old schools, our old playgrounds, and our old friends set in, but it didn't matter. Dad had decided, and whether we liked it or not, it was now out with the old and in with the new.

Our new neighborhood was named Newburg. A group of Germans had settled this community, which started out as a small village in the 1800s. Later, freed slaves Henry and Eliza Tevis purchased forty acres of land at Indian Trail and Newburg Road, and the community began to grow. A historical marker for Newburg is located at Petersburg Road and Indian Trail, commemorating this legacy. Even to this day, Newburg remains a predominantly Black area.

It took a little time for us to adjust to Newburg. For the first time, we were not living close to grandparents, aunts, uncles, or cousins. Our family had always had a tendency to cherish one another and enjoy spending time together. My nephew Courtney Montgomery spent much of his life living with my parents, so he is more like a brother than a nephew.

I was around eight years old when we moved, and I immediately began attending Newburg Elementary and Junior High School. Little did I realize there was another kind of school waiting for me, not very far from our house. It was the Newburg Apostolic Church Sunday school, and it would shape my family's life and mine forever.

When we first moved, the rural area looked somewhat deserted, compared to Louisville. We needed something to do. As I said earlier, as kids we thought we would have many farm animals, like cows and even horses that we could ride. Although some in the community did raise many different animals, we hardly had any, usually a few chickens and a pig or two. An older man in the neighborhood by the name of Shed Berry had a horse and wagon. He would come down the street from time to time, which was exciting for us back then. As I got older, I realized that the long hours and hard work my father did as a concrete finisher didn't leave him much time to raise animals.

After moving to Newburg, my sisters, brothers, and I began attending the Sunday school at Newburg Apostolic Church, a holiness assembly founded around 1948. We were among the first children to make up the Sunday-school class. The pastor of the church was Mattie Holland, an anointed and truly spirit-filled woman of God. She was a missionary, a wise woman of faith, and a clearly dedicated disciple of Jesus Christ.

The Lord called Pastor Holland to start a work in the small hamlet known as Newburg. At first the members of Newburg began having Bible studies and meetings in the yards of some of the members. It wasn't long before the following grew, and the congregation erected a small block church building. Pastor Holland had to face many detractors, but she persevered, and God was faithful. Hundreds of souls have been saved because of the work of this pioneer woman of God. Her husband and sons firmly supported her for years, and today, the church is thriving under her son Elder Waverly Holland.

Little did my parents know when we moved to Newburg that God's plan included bringing us into this marvelous place of worship under such an anointed woman of God. Pastor Holland loved children, and she nurtured all those in the church. I thank God for Pastor Mattie Holland. She helped instill spirituality in us, which is invaluable to a child of God.

One of Pastor Mattie Holland's favorite songs was "He Was There All the Time," which she asked my mother to sing on many occasions. My mother sang in the choir for years. She was a wonderful gospel vocalist who really believed the songs she sang, and you could tell. They were a testament to her faith in and devotion to the Lord. She was a faithful missionary and served as the missionary department's secretary for many years.

My dad could get very excited about church too, and he didn't let anything hold him back. Dad would get emotional about the Word of God. He enjoyed listening to great preachers like Dr. Johnny "the Walking Bible" James of Springfield, Ohio, and the prince of preachers, the late bishop Morris Golder. I think his favorite preacher may have been Bishop Paul A. Bowers of Cincinnati, Ohio. Dad had great faith and liked to sing gospel songs while working or just sitting around the house. After he got sick and before he passed away, he would always say, "Just call on Jesus; he will answer prayer." My wife remembered and repeated those words of faith when she was going through her illness, and God miraculously healed her of cancer. What a mighty God we serve!

Growing up in Newburg, I didn't usually have the opportunity to play with my two older brothers. Whenever I tried to follow them, they would always tell me to go home. They and their friends felt I was too young to tag along, but I was too old to hang out with my two younger brothers, who were six and seven years my junior. The move had started to change us. Therefore, God would have to give me some playmates my own age, and it was not long before he did just that.

My parents had told us we would get used to Newburg. They knew that all of us would easily make more friends and that everything would be okay. They were right. In almost no time, I became friends with my neighbors who were closer to my age and lived only a few houses down from us.

First I became close to the Seay family. They had moved to Newburg from Montgomery, Alabama, just three years before we arrived, and I believe God orchestrated the move. I was at their house so much that some folks in the community probably thought I was a Seay instead of a Northington, and the Seays' parents, Mr. Fletcher and Mrs. Pearlie, probably felt as if they had an adopted son.

Mr. Fletcher and Mrs. Pearlie Seay were good, Christian parents who always treated me with the same love and respect they did their own children. They had one girl, Rosa Etta, and six boys, Fletcher Jr., Marshall, Will, Haywood, Artis, and Tony. Mr. Fletcher was a concrete finisher as my father was, so they often worked together. Mrs. Seay was like another mother to me, always asking if I needed anything and always offering me a meal. Since they were only three houses down the street, my parents had no problem with it. They usually knew where I was if they wanted to find me.

I did just about everything with the Seays, including playing football. We hung out a lot together, especially in Newburg Park, and we became lifelong friends. Their father was a true outdoorsman, so they grew up fishing, hunting, and camping out. We went fishing in the ponds close to our neighborhood many times, and I even went hunting with them a couple of times.

The first time I went hunting with them, they lent me one of their guns since I did not have one of my own. We went to a wooded area not far from our homes, and they gave me a quick lesson. Their instructions were perfect, and it wasn't long before I shot my first rabbit, but when it kept moving, I was about to shoot it again or hit it with the gun when they yelled, "Stop! Stop!" They warned me that it was not safe to use a shotgun to hit a dying rabbit. They had forgotten to tell me about that part earlier, but it all worked out fine.

For a young boy, your first hunting trip is exciting, scary, and fun all at the same time. Friends and experiences like that don't fade from your memory very fast, and you don't want them to. The Seays were positive role models for me. They were instrumental in my development.

Tragically, Mr. Fletcher Seay stuck a nail in his foot in a work-related accident and died of the resulting infection. This was devastating to us all, especially to his family, but they courageously pulled together and persevered, with Will taking on the leadership role although he was only fourteen years old at the time.

Another neighbor and close friend was George Woodford. The Woodfords lived three houses down in the other direction and had four kids: Mary, George, Jimmy, and Ann. George was my good buddy, but at age thirteen he died from a ruptured appendix. Losing a close childhood friend is something you never really get over. To me, as a young teenager, George's death was tragic, a devastating loss. On the positive side, I will always remember the great blessing George's family received when his older sister, Mary, accepted Jesus Christ into her life. Mary said the example of my mom's life had led her to accept the Lord into her own life. The angels in heaven rejoiced on that day. "Likewise, I say unto you, there is joy in the presence of the angels of God over one sinner that repenteth" (Luke 15:10 KJV). Now that doesn't negate the pain of losing George, but in the final analysis, every soul that has been snatched from the hand of the enemy gives us reason to rejoice, despite life's setbacks.

Another family we were close to was the Harpers. There were three older siblings, Al, Mary, and Lee, and several younger ones. I was closer to Lee because he was in my Sunday-school class and later we played together on the Broadmoor baseball team. Lee lived a few miles from us in the Broadmoor subdivision, and his dad repaired televisions and radios for almost everyone in Newburg. We always wanted to treat Lee well so his dad would repair our television and get it back to us quickly. Televisions back then were not very dependable, with the tubes burning out all the time. Lee was also a great guy, and we have remained friends for life. We are also now brothers in the church and former coworkers.

Then there was the Unseld family, who became some of the best friends anyone could ever have. They had five boys and two girls, George, Sandra,

Charles Jean, Westley, Reginald, Robert, and Isaac. I can't even measure the impact the Unselds had on my life. When we were not playing out in the streets in front of the Seay house, we could be found down the street in front of the Unseld house, in their backyard, or at Newburg Park playing basketball, baseball, or football. I became lifelong friends with all the boys in these families.

If you are a true basketball fan, the name Unseld is probably familiar. Westley "Wes" Unseld starred at Seneca High School and went on to play at the University of Louisville, beginning in 1965. Wes enjoyed an illustrious NBA career with the Baltimore/Capital/Washington Bullets and was inducted into the Naismith Memorial Basketball Hall of Fame in 1988.

The Los Angeles Lakers drafted his older brother George, a star athlete at Seneca and at the University of Kansas. Before his premature death in 2010, George had a long and productive career as an educator, administrator, basketball coach, and Louisville city council member. When he took over as head basketball coach at Seneca in 1967, George made history as the state's first Black coach in a major sport at a predominantly white high school, according to a 2010 story in the *Louisville Courier-Journal*.

All the boys were tall and gifted in basketball, especially Wes, who was listed as six feet, seven inches and 245 pounds during his pro career. The two Unseld sisters were good athletes also and could really play softball.

Mrs. Unseld, the matriarch of the family, had a career with the Jefferson County Board of Education. Friends and family affectionately knew Charles Unseld, the patriarch, as "Big Charles." I always called him Mr. Unseld out of respect. He was an activist and a pillar of the community. He was an influential man who truly loved his family and the people of Newburg. He worked tirelessly to make life better for everyone. The local politicians viewed Mr. Unseld as a man who could get things done. If anyone could get a road paved or a streetlight installed, it was Mr. Unseld. He was instrumental in keeping Newburg Park jumping with baseball and other exciting events. He installed a basketball goal in his backyard, and we would often play there or at the outdoor courts at Newburg School. After they built my high school, Thomas Jefferson, Mr. Unseld and George helped build the concession stand for our football field. The Unselds were great citizens in our community, and everyone thought highly of them.

One of the most exciting and gratifying times for us was when Mr. Unseld was given some used football equipment by Central High School (the "colored" school). We had never used cleats, helmets, or any type of football gear before. When we received the news that Mr. Unseld had the gear, we swiftly made a beeline to the Unselds' house to stake our claim. Once we arrived, our hearts skipped a beat. Wow! There it was. Right in front of our eyes were all kinds of good things, including pads, jerseys, and pants.

Some of the equipment was dated and worn, but at the time that did not bother us. As far as we were concerned, that equipment was brand new. I picked out a pair of high-top running shoes, some hip pads, a shirt, and pants. I left that garage wearing a big smile and feeling very proud of my first football gear. As soon as I got home, I took a pair of scissors and cut the high-tops down. The next day, when we got on the field, it seemed like that gear made us play better than ever before. It is funny how a small gesture gave us such great pride and confidence. I will always remember that day.

One of my first experiences when we moved to Newburg was going to watch girls play fast-pitch softball. In the summer, Newburg Park was the place to be. I spent a lot of time there. The young men would also have some great fast-pitch softball games against teams from other African American communities. I will never forget the hot competition and the thrill of watching all the great athletes. Sometimes it was hard to sleep, knowing you would be going up against teams from Fort Hill, Smoketown, Parkland, Jeffersontown, and Berrytown-Griffeytown. Man, oh man, I can still feel it. Those were some real rivalries.

I remember watching a fast-pitch men's softball game between Newburg and Fort Hill. I know softball bases are closer than in baseball, but this one young man was so quick that when he hit a grounder, he would be crossing first base before the Newburg fielder could field and throw the ball. We all wanted to know who he was and learned he was Sherman Lewis, the All-State football and track star from duPont Manual High School. He later became an All-American halfback at Michigan State University and one of the first African American offensive coordinators in the National Football League. I would later hear myself being compared to Sherman Lewis when Purdue University tried to recruit me. Knowing the kind of great football player he was, I felt good about the comparison. Great athletes like that were tremendous role models to my friends and me.

Besides playing some very competitive basketball games with my friends, another favorite pastime was watching some of the greatest basketball played anywhere, right there on those Newburg basketball courts. I am proud that my community could claim the first two African American "Mr. Basketball" players in the state of Kentucky, Mike Redd and Wes Unseld. On many days, Mike and Wes hooked up with Wes's older brother, George; Mike's brother, Robert Redd; and David Cosby, another All-State player from Seneca. Those five joined forces with some of the other great neighborhood players to form a team, and they played against some of the best players in the city, such as Central High School greats like Bill Bradley, who went on to play for the Kentucky Colonels, a professional American Basketball Association (ABA) team that played in Louisville. Male High School had an All-State player and future Harlem Globetrotter Dallas Thornton. Occasionally, players from other states, such as Spencer Haywood and Ralph Sampson (both of whom went on to play in the NBA), would come through and play a few games. So would some of the other Kentucky Colonels players, like Ron Thomas, who was from Newburg and played at the University of Louisville. We would not have been surprised if the Colonels' ABA All-Star center, Artis Gilmore, came by to watch, if not play. It seemed as if the games would go on for hours at a time, and we never got enough. It was something to behold.

One of the greatest summer basketball events in Louisville and many other communities is the annual Dirt Bowl, currently played at Shawnee Park in Louisville but originally played at Algonquin Park in Louisville's West End. I am proud to say I played on the Newburg team that won the very first official Dirt Bowl championship in the early 1970s. These were awesome games to behold, some of the greatest ball games anywhere in the state, if not in the country. As a matter of fact, I once read an online ESPN article that said that basketball on the playgrounds is dying. The article talked about how Julius Erving and other NBA greats once played hoops on the playgrounds throughout the country. That's where he shucked the nickname given him by the fans at Rucker Park in New York, "the Claw," and named himself "the Doctor." The article mentioned that fans had sat on rooftops and climbed trees to see him play in the Dirt Bowl games, but now those days have faded away. Star athletes just don't want to play on the outside playgrounds any longer. They have too much to lose and nothing to gain.

That same article mentioned that the stars came out to play on the playgrounds in DC, Baltimore, and Los Angeles. Louisville was also included in the article, which noted that Artis "A Train" Gilmore would pull up in his fancy car while still wearing a fancy suit, just to play ball. The article also mentioned a story that is still circulating in Louisville—after more than two decades—about how a teenage Darrell Griffith, the Louisville All-American and NBA All-Star, drove the lane and dunked on the 7–2 Gilmore as the crowd went wild. I used to feel bad about the time a junior high school–aged Griffith dunked on me in a Dirt Bowl game, but hearing the Gilmore story definitely takes away some of the pain.

At Newburg Park, a director from the county parks and recreation department would oversee the kids' recreation activities during the summer. Several people held the job over the years. One of my all-time favorites was Mrs. Anna Tinker, mother of my good friends Jeffrey, Duke, and George Tinker. Mrs. Anna was one of the nicest and most people-oriented persons you could ever meet. She loved her job and loved all the kids who came to Newburg Park. She helped make our summer experience truly enjoyable.

As a young boy growing up in the 1950s, I had a deep love for baseball. I had a lot of "favorite" sports figures, but I was probably most impressed and influenced by the Cubs' first baseman and shortstop Ernie Banks, along with Willie "Say Hey Kid" Mays and Henry "Hammerin' Hank" Aaron. I believe that if I had concentrated and trained more and not played college football, I could have played professional baseball.

Louisville is where the legendary Louisville Slugger baseball bat is made, and during the spring and summer in Newburg Park, baseball was king. We loved our city, and we are still proud of the sports legends that it has produced, but when it came to baseball, every Little League player wanted to be like the man from Georgia, Jackie Robinson.

Most people know that Major League Baseball was segregated and that Jackie Robinson was the first Black baseball player to break the color barrier. I like to remember the teammate who befriended Jackie and assisted him in being successful in the major leagues. He was a young southern white man who became a Major League Baseball Hall of Famer: Harold Peter Henry "Pee Wee" Reese.

Pee Wee was born on July 23, 1918, in Ekron, Kentucky. He was a great athlete who played shortstop for the Brooklyn Dodgers, which later became the Los Angeles Dodgers. It was a blessing for baseball that he and Jackie Robinson played together. After Jackie joined the Dodgers in 1947, they went to Cincinnati, Ohio, for a game, and during pregame warm-ups, the fans were heckling him. Pee Wee, the captain of the team, walked over to Jackie, engaged him in conversation, and put his arm around Jackie's shoulder in a gesture of support that silenced the crowd.

Because of Pee Wee Reese, Jackie Robinson was able to endure the racial slurs and attacks, and he went on to become a baseball legend. Pee Wee showed Blacks that not everybody in the world of baseball was racist. There was hope, and by supporting his friend Jackie, Pee Wee championed that hope. Pee Wee was not only the captain of the 1950s' Dodgers team; he was a good-hearted, down-to-earth, fair, and wonderful human being.

Pee Wee may have been born in Ekron, but he grew up in my home-town. I believe his family moved to Louisville when he was about eight years old. Today, if you drive down East Main Street in Louisville, you can see a forty-foot banner with a picture of Jackie and Pee Wee high on the side of a building near the Louisville Slugger Field. Like me, they both played shortstop, but Jackie only played it for a little while. I loved Little League and baseball. Mr. Unseld and other men in the neighborhood would orga-nize teams for us. Whether it was Little League or high school, whenever I played, I made sure I excelled in the shortstop position, like Pee Wee.

Our baseball field was always in need of dragging, but we didn't mind as long as we could compete against the other neighborhood boys our age. Mr. Unseld would not only haul us around to various places to play ball; he would do his best to smooth out the field. He would attach some old metal bedsprings to his International truck, add concrete blocks, and have a couple of kids sit on them. Then away he would go, dragging the field to get out the rough spots. It was quite a sight to see. There were always kids yelling and cheering and a cloud of dust flying everywhere. When the dragging was complete, besides having a much better and smoother field, we also had a lot of dusty kids. We didn't mind because we always had a lot of fun laughing and riding. Overall, it was a great effort to get the field in good shape, and it was much appreciated.

I remember one occasion when the younger boys my age practiced all week to prepare for a challenge from another community, and when the other team arrived, its players were three or four years older than ours. Rather than let us play against these older boys, Wes Unseld and the older boys from Newburg stepped in and gave them a good old-fashioned beating. I wanted to play myself, but I was proud of the way the older guys came to our rescue. That was the last time those guys tried to pull anything like that on us. In Newburg, we stuck together and had great community pride.

It is a well-known fact that people love to congregate, and boys love to congregate wherever girls are. Sometimes after the ball games down at Chickasaw Park, Shawnee Park, or the Harris Recreation Center at Cotter Homes, the adults would have parties for us, and even when they didn't, we would hang out in the park, talking, laughing, and just having summer fun. Naturally, the better you played ball, the more popular you were after the games and in general. The great thing about that is, no matter where we played, plenty of pretty girls would come out, and for some reason, they really liked the boys from Newburg and Broadmoor. Nothing could make you feel better than hearing them cheering for you and calling out your name as you showed off your skills.

The boys agreed and disagreed with one another on such matters as the best teachers, the meanest principal, the best sports teams, the prettiest girls, and the fastest runners. Nobody wanted to rush home to see what was on television; after all, what could have been more enjoyable than one another's company? Unless something was wrong, all your best buddies would be there every time. They expected to see you and were glad when you came. We lived for baseball in the park and relationships. As we got older, it was not necessarily in that order. Those were great times with my friends, the crowds, the girls, the popularity, and the cheers. (Did I mention the girls?)

We were friends, real friends. We teased one another, chased one another, called one another by nicknames, and laughed. I have been called everything from Nathaniel to Nate, Nat, and even Nute.

My parents and my relatives on my father's side called me Nathaniel. My siblings called me Nay, and I was always Nate to most of my friends growing up. However, once I reached high school and started getting media publicity, somehow it became Nat, so you may see my name in various forms.

For a time, I was even called Splo, just like my dad. He got the nickname from his explosive style in football and boxing, not from being a drinker, even though some drinkers are called that. I consider the nickname an honor, except that I was only a teenager and, I promise you, at the time I was nowhere close to being as explosive on the field or in boxing as he was.

The main thing is that the other boys and I were friends, and good friends call you by the name that represents the relationship you share. Back then, it seemed as though we treasured our growing up. Our friendships were more genuine than what I see among youths today. We talked to one another. No text messages, no cell phones, and no loud music drowning out what we had to say.

It reminds me of the *Cheers* theme song. In a 2011 readers' poll in *Rolling Stone* magazine, the song was voted the best television theme of all time. There is something in it that rings true: it is always good to be "Where Everybody Knows Your Name."

I truly believe the Lord led my father to Newburg. It was a great community in which to raise a family. The neighborhoods were close-knit and had some wonderful Christian people in them. Who would have guessed that a move that started out with childhood stress and uncertainty would end up being the beginning of the good old days? There is an old African proverb that says, "It takes a village to raise a child." Don't ask me who said it or where it came from. I just know that the Newburg community was definitely a village and that all the people, families, and friends were a great influence on me as I grew up. The spiritual and natural friendships we made have resulted in many solid, godly relationships.

4

Getting Ready for Some Football

As I stated before, as a teenager I played baseball with the Newburg Tigers for a couple of years, and we had some talented teams, with players like Reginald Unseld as catcher, Gene Lewis at third base, George Lee as pitcher, and Ernest Lewis at second base, just to name a few. We normally played on the Newburg ball field, and we developed some great rivalries.

One team we played against was from the relatively new Newburg subdivision of Broadmoor. Now, it's one thing to be recognized and honored by your friends, but it is another thing when the praise comes from your rivals. In this sense, the word *rivals* does not have a negative connotation. We all went to school together, so our school spirit was intact. Broadmoor was built for African Americans around 1955 and was part of Newburg as well, although it was across Newburg Road, which became the dividing line for the kids who went to Seneca and the kids who went to Thomas Jefferson (TJ).

Since we lived in different neighborhoods, we had some hot competitions, and of course, the goal was to outplay, outscore, outclass, and outshine the boys from the other areas. Whenever we played against Broadmoor, the games were tough. One year, the process of organizing teams was in progress, but for some reason our Newburg neighborhood was slow in getting it together, and I was becoming anxious about whether I would get to play that summer.

My friends and classmates on the Broadmoor team remembered that I had been a big factor in our games against them, so we started talking about having me join them for that season. I was all for it. When we approached Mr. Cowden, he immediately agreed with the suggestion because he knew I could help make their team stronger. I was about fourteen when they asked me, and I felt proud to be drafted by Broadmoor. Their coach was Elmer Cowden. He was a good man and role model who devoted all his spare time to coaching us and treating us like members of his family. We spent so much time at his house and around his family that, in a way, I guess we were part of the family.

Playing against Broadmoor was tough, but playing with Broadmoor was fun. I still maintained my friendship with all my old Newburg teammates, and a couple of them even came over to Broadmoor to play with me. It was baseball heaven, if there is such a thing. We had some outstanding players at every position. All my buddies from the hood played: pitchers like Eddie Rudolph, Walter Parks, and George Lee; center fielder Hilton Humphrey; catcher Ricky Stone; infielders James Stallings, Freddy Cowden, and Eddie Hickerson; and me at shortstop most of the time.

We had some great teams, and we won most leagues in which we played down at Chickasaw Park. Louisville has more than 120 city parks, but somewhere around 1924, African Americans were banned from the majority of them. Before the integration of Shawnee, our leagues played at Chickasaw Park, which was just about the only park open to us for a long time. Chickasaw, like most of the major parks in Louisville, is named after Native American nations. The others include Seneca, Shawnee, Iroquois, and Cherokee. They were much larger with more attractions than Chickasaw, but we could not go to those parks. Chickasaw, which was built in an all-white neighborhood in the West End in the late 1920s, was designated for Black use only in response to outrage from Black community leaders over the segregation of the parks.

The funny thing is that at one point during segregation, Blacks could go through Shawnee Park to get to Chickasaw, but they couldn't stay and play ball there until it was finally integrated. I remember white kids throwing rocks at us whenever we walked near the Shawnee neighborhood. That didn't stop us. We threw those rocks right back. Once we were able to start playing there, we had a great time and realized what we had been missing. The park was big enough to accommodate seven or eight baseball fields.

The main field was fenced in with seating, lights, and a smooth infield, like in the major leagues. Even after integration, it was probably about seven or eight years before the majority of Blacks really felt welcome at Shawnee Park.

An amusement park, Fontaine Ferry, was right next to Shawnee, and it had roller coasters and all kinds of rides, but Blacks were not able to go there until the late 1960s. I remember the protests in front of the park during the 1960s, people holding signs condemning the discrimination that was taking place in our hometown. We were being denied our rights as citizens and taxpayers of the city of Louisville. After much prayer and suffering, all the persistence paid off, and the park was integrated. We were finally able to go to the park and enjoy the rides and festivities that we had been denied for so long.

Chickasaw became a focal point for African American families who gathered to have picnics and to play tennis and other games, especially baseball. We loved Chickasaw Park almost as much as Newburg Park and spent so many memorable days there playing baseball. Ironically, the West End neighborhood itself was integrated and by the 1970s was nearly all Black.

When the leagues started, we played against some of the teens from several of the new housing communities (Cotter Homes, Lang Homes/ Southwick, and Beecher Terrace). Some players became our good friends, like Raymond Patterson of the West End Warriors and Wilbur Hackett, June Vincent, and brothers Danny and Jerry Williams of the Brady Tigers. When we got on the field, the fans were boisterous and rabid. These were some competitive and emotionally charged games. Win or lose, we loved the competition. But we won more than we lost and still remained friends. These are memories I will cherish throughout my life.

Our team was the Broadmoor Bears, and we had some good-looking uniforms. We were great players who looked sharp. Looking good and playing well—no wonder the girls followed us.

Most of the players on our team went on to play in high school, and some played in college. Being drafted by Broadmoor was definitely one of the highlights of my teenage years. I will always remember and cherish those times with my friends.

At home on Sunday afternoons during the fall and winter months, the men of the house gathered in the front room to watch professional football on TV. My father loved football. His favorite player was James Nathaniel "Jim" Brown, the Hall of Fame fullback for the Cleveland Browns who led the league in rushing for eight years in a row. He is unquestionably the greatest running back of all time. In only nine years, he rushed for 12,312 yards and scored 106 rushing touchdowns in only 93 games. On November 4, 2010, he was chosen as the second-greatest player in the league's history by the NFL Network's series *The Top 100: NFL's Greatest Players*, produced by NFL Films.

According to fellow Hall of Famer John Mackey, the great Jim Brown once told him, "Make sure when anyone tackles you, he remembers how it hurts." I grew up watching this all-time great, and whenever he got the ball, Dad would get excited, jump up and down, and yell, "Go, Jim Brown; go, Jim Brown," and of course, Jim Brown would never disappoint him. He would run around, over, and through players, dragging them along the way as they held on for dear life. He was an extraordinary football player.

Dad was always eager to talk about football. In the middle of watching the games, he would interrupt and give us pointers on how to run the ball and avoid tacklers. He always stressed, "No matter how fast you are, always follow your blockers. Try always to move in the direction opposite their blocks. This will help you avoid the opposing players until you get a chance to make your cut. When the chance comes, *boom*, you explode through the hole!"

When the game ended, I would immediately go out to meet my friends, and we would find a place to play, even in the street if there was nowhere else, and imitate our favorite players. Of course, I would always choose a running back, usually Jim Brown.

When it came to sports, my dad had a great gift of gab. Not only did he love football; he was good at it. In fact, if you wanted to know what a tremendous player he was, all you needed to do was ask him, and he would certainly tell you. Most of the time, he would tell you even if you didn't ask, but Dad was not all talk. He had plenty of witnesses to his athletic prowess, including his brothers and sisters. They would confirm his exploits. I learned a lot from watching games on television with Dad. I guess you could say he was my first coach, and his lessons stayed with me throughout my career and helped make me the player I became.

Now, if anybody had the right to give that advice, it was Dad. He had the perfect build to be a football player and had played on a local semipro team when he was young. Dad was about five feet, nine inches tall and weighed around 215 pounds, with broad shoulders and a powerful chest. His strong legs and upper arms helped make him such a dynamic and explosive player that he earned the nickname Splo.

When I was about twelve, I saw my first organized football game. It was at Seneca High School. My older brother William Jr. played junior varsity there, and he had started to build a reputation in the neighborhood. People said he was an outstanding player. I tended to believe it, but I needed to see it firsthand, so one day a group of friends and I walked to the school to see the game. That proves how badly we wanted to see the game, because the field was several miles away.

We tried to get there as fast as we could, but when we arrived, the game had already begun. Someone there told us my brother had already run back two punt returns and made two touchdowns. I remember feeling disappointed that I had missed seeing the touchdowns, but that feeling would not last long. After a short while, Seneca managed a three-and-out, and the opposing team was forced to punt the ball again. That is when I saw what everybody else had seen.

William Jr. either forgot to follow the blockers, as Dad always reminded us, or just decided to ignore that tip. Before Seneca's punt-return team could even get into formation, my brother caught that ball and took off like a jackrabbit. He ran and he ran, zigzagging down that field, bucking and weaving like a pro. William Jr. sprinted all the way for another touchdown, and the crowd went wild. That was amazing to me. I had known he was fast, but this time, it seemed as if he'd been shot out of a cannon. The opposing team had punted to my brother three times that day, and he returned all three punts for touchdowns. To me, that was sensational. I could see my brother was ready for some football. After that, they made sure to punt every ball away from my brother and completely out of bounds. That team was not taking any more chances on him returning another punt for a touchdown.

Both of my older brothers would have been great college players if they had chosen to participate. I was always impressed with how fast they could run, and the other kids in the neighborhood were impressed with their speed as well, as they often mentioned it to me. They wanted to know how we all got so fast, even my sisters. My parents told us they could run fast as well. My older brothers chose to marry and start families early in their lives. They became successful family men and Christians.

If I had not already made up my mind to play football, watching my brother that day was the deciding factor. I was still in junior high school, but at the moment, I chose football as my career. I made up my mind that I was going to play ball at Seneca High School, and after that, I wanted to become a star running back in college and play professionally in the NFL. I was thrilled, proud of my brother, and inspired as well. Through the years, remembering what my brother had done inspired me to always work hard on the field and off, in everything I chose to do. God gave me natural talent, but it was up to me to work hard enough to be the best I could be.

Often my friends and I played football with boys who were older and bigger than we were, but that didn't matter. They were not any tougher than I was, and they could not beat me at running. When I got the ball, I was usually able to gain big yardage and score a touchdown. I was very quick, agile, and elusive, and I was not prone to being injured. I think the hard work I did with Dad made me stronger and tougher than most kids were at my age, and the speed and athleticism God gave me made me a good athlete. I enjoyed the competition, so I didn't let minor details such as age and size stop me from playing.

Even though we did not have Pop Warner or the Police Activities League to regulate age, size, or weight limits, I was fast enough and tough enough to hold my own, even with the older boys. We would choose sides and play with everything we had. Back then, if we were injured, we just sucked it up and kept going. Injuries were not much of a problem. We just learned how to protect ourselves, and I loved the game so much I would play with any minor pain.

As so many coaches say, "When the going gets tough, the tough get going."

I knew from a young age I had a lot of natural talent. We usually played football wherever we found a vacant lot—beside churches, near industrial plants, anywhere. If someone ran us off one field, we would just go find another. Because of our love for the game, we did not let anything stop us.

According to experts, every year, twenty million kids sign up for baseball, soccer, football, hockey, or other league sports. Seventy percent of those kids drop out by age thirteen and never play again. Most of them quit around middle school because they say it's not fun anymore, and they don't really like the heavy focus on having to win. I'm glad nothing like that ever happened to me. At that age, I could not even imagine losing my love for the game. I loved to play, and I loved to win. Playing was always fun, even in school when it was tough. As far as I can remember, the only thing that was not fun about sports was when I couldn't play. We spent our time watching sports, playing sports, or thinking about watching and playing sports. And who can deny the benefits sports give young kids by teaching them lasting values like teamwork, discipline, character, and dedication, and showing them how to handle adversity. I learned all these lessons from participating in sandlot and organized sports. Without a doubt, athletics certainly can be a tremendous asset to the youth in our communities.

Other than my brother's performance at Seneca, I don't know exactly what made me choose football—or what makes anybody choose it, for that matter. I think it was my competitive nature. I loved to compete, and football gave me that opportunity. The camaraderie with my friends and teammates, the sheer fun of running and jumping, and the physical nature of the game all inspired me. All I know is that I just loved to play the game. I enjoyed everything about it, especially the thrill you get when making a long run, faking and breaking tackles, and, of course, scoring a touchdown. There is nothing quite like it.

Let's face it: football is tough, and the practices are tough. But that didn't bother me one bit. The tougher it got, the more I liked it. It made me feel good to play my heart out and come out with a victory. If you have a good coach, the discipline is often personal because he knows what you are capable of and expects you to give it all you have and then some. Football is definitely not the game for the faint of heart. You have to be ready for football, and if you are not, you should stay on the sidelines. It's an all-around tough sport—the only one in which every position requires you to run directly at another man and hit, grab, block, or tackle him. It is tough, but it is rewarding. The late famed Michigan State University football coach Duffy Daugherty once said, "Football isn't a contact sport. It's a collision sport. Dancing is a contact sport."

To win at all levels, coaches demand that their players work harder and do everything consistently better than the other team. That's probably why many kids drop out of sports early in life. I can truly say that I thank my family for getting me ready for football. If I have shown any discipline, knowledge of the game, love of sports, teamwork, tenacity, or good sportsmanship, it all came from my community and from my family. Football is a lot like life. You have to be dedicated and work hard. You will face times of agony and defeat, but if you get up, get going, and hold your head up, you will be victorious.

Like a coach, Dad taught us and motivated us to perform at our best. He was extremely focused. Watching him work helped me see that in every part of life, I needed to be where I was supposed to be and understand my responsibilities when I got there.

Even the not-so-good times helped shape me and get me ready for some football. Those times that the white kids threw rocks at us at Shawnee Park made me stronger and more determined. In fact, I don't remember hating white people or those kids because of their behavior. I do know that everything I went through helped prepare me for life. Even though I didn't have very much personal interaction with whites until I got into high school sports, we just weren't brought up to hate.

It took me four decades to decide to write my story. When I was asked why it had taken so long, one of the many reasons became very clear. I don't like to talk, toot my own horn, or appear to be a braggadocio. But since the person questioning me wouldn't take no for an answer, I had to be blunt. In my younger days as an athlete, I was good, very good. I was naturally fast, but I was also very quick, and in athletics, that's a tremendous asset. It is one thing to have blazing speed and another to have quick reactions, and not all fast athletes can react quickly. It may take some time for them to react, but once they do, they can turn on the speed. I had an extremely quick reaction time, which was an asset.

Besides my God-given talents and the hard work I put into improving my skills, I also had something you could not teach. I had the intelligence and the instincts, or, as they say, a nose for the game, sort of a sixth sense.

The old saying "Practice makes perfect" has much merit, but no one can get instinct through practice. It is second nature, and either you have it or you don't, and God gave it to me. It is sort of like mother wit for sports.

Instinct allowed me to run to the right hole, make the right cut, see how the play was developing, and get in position to break up a pass, make a tackle, intercept the ball, and run a punt back for a touchdown. When the defender thought he had me cornered and was in position to tackle me, I could make a cut or turn on the speed to avoid the tackle. It was as if I were saying, "Now you see me; now you don't," or "Goodbye, see you later, zoom!" Or, as one of my teammates used to say, it was like an explosion, leaving the other player nothing to grab but air.

I ran with such smooth and effortless motion that I made it look too easy, I guess. I was really running hard and giving it all I had. My style made it seem like I was barely moving when I was going at high speed. I believe the results were proof of that. One thing is certain: I ran for many touchdowns throughout my career, and I am proud to say I was never once caught from behind.

People who are familiar with my game say that whenever I ran, I never appeared to be running fast or putting much effort into it. When I watch tapes of myself, I do seem to be running with ease. They say I ran with a kind of smoothness, with the grace of a swan swimming, like someone just cruising or a deer moving through its territory.

In the *Lexington Herald-Leader* article "Does Northington Glide, Lope, or Just Run?," UK backfield coach Leon Fuller said, "He runs like a racehorse, he has an easy stride, and he's fast." In the same article, Coach Charlie Bradshaw said, "More like an antelope, he takes five yards in two strides."

"He's slow like water," said fellow sophomore Stan Forston, indicating that still water runs deep and a seemingly still Nat Northington was actually flying.

Now, on the one hand, having style was a blessing, but on the other hand, I believe it was also sort of a curse. It was a blessing because I could elude tacklers or blow by them because they had misjudged my speed and quickness. When they thought they could move into position and tackle me, I could give them a Gale Sayers–type juke and change directions. It was sort of a curse, I believe, because regardless of the success I had, the coaches had even higher expectations. I always, always gave 100 percent—my forty-yard-dash time spoke for itself—and I couldn't help that I made everything look easy.

Here is what the UK media guide said my sophomore year: "Sophomore Nat Northington seems to be the best cornerback since Bradshaw has been at UK."

Bradshaw indicated that opponents would be reluctant to kick the ball to Dicky Lyons Sr. or me and would rather kick it out of bounds for fear that we would run it back for a touchdown. This actually happened in our game at Auburn University. Dicky ran the first punt back for a touchdown, and when I came in for the next punt return, the Auburn punter kicked the ball out of bounds. Bradshaw had seen me run back several punts for touchdowns during spring practice, so he knew the potential of our punt-return team.

In track and field, I was one of the top hurdlers in the state as a junior and senior, winning my district in the 120-yard highs and 180-yard lows, as well as running on the 880-yard (4 × 220) and mile (4 × 440) relay teams. I often ran in all those running events and also participated in the high jump and broad jump, all in the same track meet. You don't do that without being a top athlete in excellent shape. Most people could not do that in a week, much less all in the same day. Then I would follow that up the next day by playing seven innings of shortstop on my high school baseball team.

To do all that takes strength, stamina, and a whole lot of heart. Nobody ever questioned my heart. I always left it on the field. I was just never one to back down from a sports challenge, and although my style seemed smooth and easy, I was working as hard as I could. I just made it look easy.

Newburg was a Black elementary and junior high school when my sisters, brothers, and I started going there after moving from Parkland (Little Africa). At that time, I was in third grade. The Black high school kids had to travel about fifteen miles all the way downtown to Louisville Central High School or thirty-five miles to Lincoln Institute in Shelby County, Kentucky. There were no other choices because of segregation. I think every city in the country had a Central High School.

After the 1954 Supreme Court decision on integration, two schools on the eastern fringe of Louisville, Seneca High School and Goldsmith Elementary and Junior High School, integrated, and they started accepting the Black kids from Newburg. After that, Newburg became an elementary school only. All the Black junior high kids, including my siblings and some of my friends, started going to the integrated schools, leaving me behind at Newburg.

Seneca was a relatively new high school, but after the Black kids from the Newburg community began going there, it was not long before the school won back-to-back state championships in basketball in 1963 and 1964. That's when Newburg resident Mike Redd became the first African American to be named Mr. Basketball in the state of Kentucky, in 1963. The very next year, Wes Unseld led Seneca to its second state championship and was also named Mr. Basketball by the Kentucky High School Athletic Association. The Kentucky Colonels of the American Basketball Association also tried to lure Wes from the University of Louisville during his junior year by offering him a reported $500,000. This was long before today's one-year-and-done college players and before kids could go straight from high school to the NBA. The ABA was trying to build its star power. Wes did not accept the ABA offer; he stayed in school to complete his senior year. In 1968, Kentucky drafted Wes, but he was also the second overall player taken in the NBA draft, and he signed with the Baltimore Bullets, which later moved to Washington.

At that time, Wes Unseld was the only NBA player other than Wilt Chamberlain to win Rookie of the Year and Most Valuable Player in the same season. Wes was one of the key contributors when the Bullets beat the Seattle SuperSonics to win the NBA championship in 1978. In 1996, he was named one of the NBA's fifty greatest players of all time.

Besides Wes Unseld, the NBA drafted two other players who had played at Seneca and lived in my Newburg community: George Unseld, by the Los Angeles Lakers, and Mike Redd, by the Boston Celtics. Three fellow alumni from Western Kentucky, Clem Haskins, Greg Smith, and Jim McDaniels, made it to the NBA.

During his career, Wes played against Kareem Abdul-Jabbar, Julius "Doctor J" Erving, George "the Ice Man" Gervin, and many other legends of the game.

Before all that, though, we would all just hang out in the park or in the Unselds' backyard, shooting baskets. During those backyard days and in high school, I was a good basketball player. I was named honorable mention All-State for two years in a row.

I was an excellent ball handler and good scorer, and I was really fast. At least I thought I was. If I got lucky, I could make a basket or two against Wes back in the day, but over time, it became obvious that I was nowhere close to the caliber of player he was.

I remember one occasion when we were playing in their backyard. Wes stepped in front of me, to try to guard me, but I threw a head fake and then blasted around him to attempt a layup. The lane was clear, and it seemed as if I had left Wes a mile away, standing where he was, but when I reached the basket, Wes came from out of nowhere and blocked my shot. The funny thing is that no matter how fast I got away from him, he could block my shot over and over again. After a while, I figured he was just letting me get around him, just so he could do practice his shot-blocking technique. He should give me some credit for his development because I gave him a lot of practice. He was a tremendous player and, like all the Unseld family, a great person. Two of his younger brothers, Robert and Isaac, were my teammates in high school, and they helped TJ win the regional championship and advance to the state tournament.

Some years ago, I watched a television show called *The Wonder Years*. In it, a boy named Kevin told the story of the good times and the not-so-good times that he had growing up in the 1960s. Even though I wasn't a regular viewer, the few times I saw the show I heard him say things that rang true for me. In one episode, for example, after explaining that he had grown up in a place no different from any other, he said, "And the thing is, after all these years, I still look back . . . with wonder."

The most desirable school in Kentucky, as far as I was concerned, was Seneca. My heart's desire was to go there when I reached the seventh grade and play ball like my brother, but a not-so-funny thing happened every time I got closer to my dream of going to Seneca. Near the end of every school year, when it was time for me to advance, Newburg added another grade to its class load. When I reached seventh grade, they added a seventh grade. When I advanced to eighth grade, they added an eighth. When it was time for me to go to ninth grade? You guessed it. They added a ninth grade.

Each addition pushed Seneca further and further out of my reach. It was almost as if somebody had carefully planned for me not to set foot inside Seneca as a student. To make absolutely sure I never made it there, they built another high school for students my age to attend. They called it Thomas Jefferson High. We called it "TJ." It was located just a couple of miles from my home and right on the fringes of the Newburg community. I had looked forward to going to Seneca High School, but it was clear I would never go there.

Two of my friends who had brothers who attended Seneca Junior High. The three of us decided to try out for Seneca's junior varsity football team. That shows you how badly I wanted to play football at Seneca. Although I was still a student at Newburg, I wasn't going to let that stop me from trying to get on that team. I put on my sweats and went to the field to wait for practice to begin. When the players came out of the locker room and went to the field, my friends and I joined in the warm-ups before practice started. Needless to say, this lasted for only a short time before the coaches noticed that I (and a couple of others) didn't belong there, and they made us leave the field.

We were disappointed that we could not stay but happy that we had spent some time on the field and participated in several exercises, even though we did not go to the school. Although our first attempt at playing organized football was not successful, that did not discourage us. We had had our first taste of high school football, and we were even more determined than ever, so we returned to our sandlots and played harder than we had in the past to prepare for our next opportunity.

We knew that the next time we stepped back on a field—as high school football players several years later—we would be successful. We would be so good that nobody would ask us to get off the field.

That day was forever stuck in our memories, and we laughed about it for many years.

Meanwhile, it looked as if I would be stuck at Newburg forever. By seventh grade, I was thinking, What could possibly happen to fix this? Then suddenly, like a direct answer to my question, a new physical education teacher and coach walked into the gym. His name was Robert Graves.

Coach Graves had recently graduated from Kentucky State College, a historically Black school. He had played on the Louisville Central High School basketball teams that had won the Negro National Championships in 1955 and 1956. This was before the Black high schools could compete

against their white counterparts for the state basketball championship. He
had also played for Kentucky Hall of Fame coach Willie Keen and gone on
to become a Kentucky Hall of Famer himself.

One day, Coach Graves informed us that he was going to start a junior
high school basketball team and that he would be holding tryouts. As you
can imagine, I was elated that we were going to have a basketball team.
During the tryouts, I thought I had done a good job of hustling, defending,
and shooting free throws. Even though I felt I had played well and made a
good showing, when it was all over, I was still anxious while waiting for the
coach to call the names of the players who had made the team.

He called several players over, and then he paused for several seconds,
looking down at the piece of paper in his hand. I would have given anything
to make my name magically appear on that paper, or just to get a look at it.
One or two players stood, but most of us just lay on the floor. It was so quiet
that I was surprised we couldn't hear one another's thoughts. I remember
lying there, staring at the ceiling. It seemed like an eternity, but finally, he
called my name: "Northington!"

Ha! There it was. When I heard that, I could have jumped up and
shouted. I felt like screaming out "Woo-hoo!," but instead I just breathed
a deep, slow sigh of relief.

One of the first things Coach Graves did was tell us we were going to
get new basketball shoes. We were accustomed to having assorted kinds of
off-brand shoes, but we were now going to get "Chuck Taylor" Converse
All Stars. I didn't know a "Chuck Taylor" All Star from any other all-star.
I had noticed how good Coach Graves's shoes looked, but I didn't know
what they were. Coach told us that he could get the shoes at a discount
and that every player would need to bring him $9.50 so he could purchase
the new shoes. At first I didn't know where in the world I was going to
get the $9.50, but with odd jobs and my parents' help, I was able to come
up with it.

We all turned in our money and waited as patiently as we could for
the shoes. A few days later, Coach Graves came to practice with all these
boxes of brand-new "Chuck Taylor" Converse All Stars. I had chosen the
low-cut model, and man, when I opened the box and saw these top-of-the-
line shoes, I broke out in the biggest smile. We all broke a record getting

dressed to go practice. Coach said that he had never seen us move as fast or jump as high as we did that day.

Basketball season started, and man, did we have some kind of a team. Coach Graves was an outstanding player, and he was a great coach. He taught us the fundamentals of the game and the work ethic that would set the stage for the future and the great teams we would have at Thomas Jefferson High School. I started as a guard, and we had several outstanding players. Ron Gathright and Jim DeWalt, who were about six feet three and six feet two, respectively, played center and forward. They were my teammates throughout our junior high and high school basketball careers. All three of us would become All-State basketball players in high school. Gathright played in the annual Kentucky–Indiana All-Star game.

At Newburg, we had three things in our favor: speed, quickness, and pressing defense. Because of this, not only were we undefeated in the seventh grade but our games usually ended in blowouts. For the next three years, our team was the talk of Newburg. It seemed as though everybody in the neighborhood who didn't work during the day would come to Newburg School to see us play. By the time we got to the eighth and ninth grades, we were playing in gyms that were filled to capacity, which was unusual for a junior high school team. Because people had heard about us, there would usually be standing room only. Those who couldn't get into the gym would stand outside, looking through the windows. We had some terrific games against some of the best talent in the city, and we usually won those games. In fact, I don't believe we lost more than two or three games during the entire three years we played at Newburg.

In our last year at Newburg, Coach Graves took us over to Thomas Jefferson to play in its new gym. It was a brand-new school with a beautiful gymnasium. Of course, we won the game easily, and the TJ head coach, Bob Hearin, came over to me after the game and said I was going to be his starting guard the next year. I was surprised that he was making plans for me to play for TJ. I didn't think he even knew who I was, but I did have a pretty good game that day, scoring on some dandy drives, hitting several jumpers, and playing great pressing defense as usual. I hadn't realized it at the time, but I later learned that the TJ basketball and football coaches had been coming over to our games and practices, scouting us so they could be prepared to utilize our skills once we got to high school. They became aware of the tremendous talent that existed at Newburg, and they couldn't wait for us to graduate and go to TJ. Because it was a new school, it did not yet have a varsity athletic program, but it would not take long for it to make a mark in Louisville. Once we made it to TJ, the school's athletic program would put it on the map and make us known throughout the state of Kentucky.

Before we moved on to high school, Coach Graves called the team to the gym and wished us well. He thanked us for all we had accomplished at Newburg and told us he expected great things from us in high school. He said he was proud of all his players, and of course, we were thankful and blessed to have had him as our coach. None of us could have known at the time that during our senior year at TJ, in 1966, we would play against our old Newburg coach for the regional championship. This, of course, was after he had become head coach at Central High School. We beat the Central team in a barn burner and went on to play in the Kentucky High School Athletic Association Sweet Sixteen State Basketball Championship.

Thanks to Coach Graves, my basketball years at Newburg were the best anybody could have ever had. Thanks to the Jefferson County School Board, I never made it to Seneca. Everything turned out well, very well. God blessed me with a wonderful experience during my junior high school days at Newburg. The fact is, if I had gone to Seneca instead of Thomas Jefferson, my teammates and I would not have been able to make names for ourselves the way we did. As far as I'm concerned, God had it all in control. "And we know that all things work together for good to them that love God, to them who are the called according to his purpose" (Romans 8:28 KJV).

I am grateful for the years the Lord allowed me to attend the elementary and junior high school in Newburg. Some outstanding Black teachers, coaches, and principals nurtured us and challenged us to be good students and productive citizens in our community and country. With their direction and support, I was blessed to be one of the top students at Newburg, consistently making the honor roll and becoming a top achiever. This laid the foundation for me to compete and achieve success throughout high school, college, and my professional career. I wouldn't trade anything for the years I spent at Newburg, and the school song reflects the sentiments of my heart:

> Newburg, oh Newburg, oh how we love you so,
> Our love for you will always forever grow.
> We are proud of our school,
> Self-control is our rule,
> In the classrooms,
> In the lunchroom, gym, halls, and everywhere.

Even in the school song, our teachers and administration were preparing us to be men and women of dignity.

5

Getting in the Game

Despite the success of our Newburg basketball team and my excitement to be on the basketball court, my heart was set on playing football. Basketball was good, but football was my life. I guess it was just in my blood. There was never any doubt in my mind that I would play football, first in high school and college and later, I hoped, in the NFL. That was my dream, and I was prepared to do everything within my power to achieve it.

In tenth grade I attended Thomas Jefferson High School (TJ). It was a new, integrated high school, and at times I joked that they had probably built it just so I couldn't go to Seneca. Since Thomas Jefferson only went to the tenth grade, my grade was the highest in the school. After I started going to TJ, it wasn't long before I forgot about Seneca. Here was a brand-new school just a few miles from my house, and I could continue going to school with many of my old Newburg friends and teammates.

Jim Gray, a future Kentucky Hall of Fame coach, was my football coach at TJ, and he wasted no time preparing us to compete at the highest level. The summer before I was to enroll at TJ, he invited all the athletes from Newburg who were interested in playing football to participate in a summer conditioning program at the school. We didn't know what to expect, but it didn't take long to find out. Coach Gray knew what it would take to get us ready, and it was no walk in the park. It wasn't long before we were running in the sandboxes, lifting weights, and going through agility and conditioning drills.

He worked us as we had never been worked before. I had thought I was in good shape, but believe me, being in basketball or baseball shape and being in football shape are entirely different things. I was thankful for the work I had done with Dad all those years, working in the heat and lifting heavy concrete, pushing wheelbarrows, carrying cement blocks and bricks, and digging footers. Because of that I was able to endure more than the kids who had had little or no work experience.

Coach Gray kept us motivated by sharing some of the football plays that we would be using in the fall. I couldn't wait, and I am sure he felt the same way. He had high expectations for the team because he knew he was getting some great athletes from Newburg to add to the players he had had on his junior high team the previous year. By the end of summer, we were ready to play some football.

We were restricted from playing varsity football because we did not have juniors or seniors in our school, but that didn't matter. I was thrilled to get an opportunity to play organized football and other sports on this level for the first time. We played a junior varsity schedule.

When the coaches and team managers handed out new football equipment the first day of practice, we were excited. I had never had anything like it before. We had gotten a taste of new equipment when we played basketball at Newburg, but this was my first experience with brand-new football gear. All the practice gear and clothing that they gave us was brand-spanking new—helmets, shoulder pads, pants, jerseys, cleats, and even socks—and this was just for practice. I couldn't imagine what the game uniforms would be like, but when we got those, we were full of pride. I thought, "They must have a lot of money over here." I was overwhelmed and could not believe it was really happening. I don't know what I had expected, but this was far from it. It reminded me of the time Mr. Unseld gave us that used football equipment that felt like new to us.

My first day on the field took me back to the day I had seen my brother run for Seneca. This is what I had been working for, and that day was here. It felt better than any Christmas I ever had. "Now," I thought, "just give me the ball, and watch what I can do." But to my surprise, the coaches put me at the wide-receiver position. I knew of some outstanding receivers in the pros, but I was disappointed because I had been grooming myself for a halfback position (or tailback, as they started calling it at that time) since my sandlot days. I hadn't considered that the coaches had never seen me play, so they didn't know what position would be best for the team or me, and they already had players at that position from the previous year. I knew I would have to show them what I could do.

Today, in the higher levels of sports, if you've got the skills and talent, the coaches will pretty much allow you to try out for the position you want (at least in the beginning), but in the 1960s, that was not the case. Back in those days, at all levels of sports and especially in high school, many coaches would play Blacks only in certain positions. Blacks had to compete against one another for playing time. The white players did not have to compete against the Blacks just to get in the game. This was the case in college as well, and even in the pros. For the most part, Black players did not get to play quarterback. There were some exceptions, of course, and I am aware of at least one Black quarterback in 1964, Garnett Phelps at Male High School, but that was extremely rare.

I soon found out that Coach Gray was a man ahead of his time in the way he coached and the way he treated Black players and everyone in general. He did not tolerate any racial mistreatment in any way and was a champion of integration. Coach Gray played the best players, regardless of ethnicity. I'm sure he probably took some flak from parents, boosters, and school administrators, but he was his own man, a maverick, and he stuck to his guns. Because of his convictions, he was rewarded not only with some outstanding teams but with players and fans who respected and loved him. However, we were only repaying him for his commitment to us, and I believe we had better teams and all became better human beings because of it.

He treated everyone with dignity, respect, and fairness. He expected the same from all his coaches, and I believe his strong example and attitude had a positive influence on the school administration as well. Coach Gray would not accept any of his players being mistreated by anyone and would go out of his way to ensure fair treatment from teachers, boosters, and even the board of education. He fought for us in every area, even academically. Because of the care and attention he showed, many of his players blossomed as fantastic football players who became outstanding men.

Athletics took up a lot of time, but that did not keep me from maintaining my academic standing. I had excellent study habits because of the nurturing of my mom, and I was able to maintain a high grade point average in spite of the rigors of playing and practicing sports every day of the week. God blessed me with a good mind, and my parents instilled in me the desire to get an education and work hard. In fact, I took as much pride in being an excellent student and achieving at the highest level academically as I did in being an athlete. The hard work and focus allowed me to succeed in both areas of my life.

I must also give credit for my success to my sister Rose. She was a role model for me throughout my school years. She was a straight-A student at Seneca High School who received an academic scholarship to Catherine Spalding College. She became the first in our family to attend college, and she graduated with honors. Rose was also in the same high school graduating class as Wes Unseld. I learned how to apply myself and become an outstanding student from the positive example, leadership, and support she exhibited on a daily basis.

Going to TJ was my first experience attending an integrated school. It didn't seem to matter to me at the time, but for some reason, I noticed that at TJ, all the coaches were white. This was a new experience for me since all the coaches at Newburg had been Black, as had all my Little League coaches. There were two Black teachers at TJ, but our principal, W. D. Bruce, and all the other school administrative staff and counselors were white. I remember the school having two Black custodians out of a total of six, and there was an African American member of the cafeteria staff, Mrs. Josephine Thomas. I didn't know what to expect, but from what I can remember, I didn't have any apprehension. I simply took it all in stride.

I had played in a few games against white kids in junior high school and in Little League baseball, but this was my first experience playing on an integrated team. But remember, this was not at all unusual for the 1960s in Louisville, Kentucky—as integration of the schools had taken place only a few years prior to this time. My brothers and sisters had started attending an integrated Goldsmith Elementary and Seneca High School five or six years before, and they hadn't experienced any unusual problems. Naturally, there were some rumblings in the community about various issues and concerns, and that was to be expected, but I am not aware of any major problems. I am sure the success of the athletic programs at Seneca was instrumental in bringing the races together and easing most of the racial tension. It didn't take long for me to realize that I was welcomed with open arms. On and off the field, we established good positive relationships with our classmates and teammates. Similar to the situation at Seneca, I believe the success of our athletic teams was a big factor in the development of those friendly relationships. I don't know if that was because the coach set the tone or because they needed us to help them win. But I believe it was because of the content of their character.

I don't know about other schools, but at TJ, it did not seem as though we were in the 1960s. My coaches, teachers, and white classmates always treated my Black classmates and me with respect. Oh, there were occasional instances of friction, but those were exceptions. This worked well for me because my parents had always taught me to treat everyone with courtesy and respect, the way I would want to be treated.

TJ had a student ratio of about 80 percent white and 20 percent Black, but our basketball and football teams were more than 40 percent African American, unlike those of most schools in Louisville. I believe the racial atmosphere at TJ was better than elsewhere in the city of Louisville and the state of Kentucky during this time. Despite the racial differences, some white families supported us very well. For example, we were often invited to the home of Mr. and Mrs. Reisser, along with some of our white teammates, like Bob Redman and Gale Daniels, for cookouts and pickup basketball games. The Reisser family even opened up their home to host our senior prom breakfast. They showed us tremendous love and treated us like members of their own family. That was unheard of in the South. Coach Gray would often let us take his Corvette Stingray to the store to pick up cigars for him to chew on. He was quite a coach and a good man.

Any negative racial incidents we had usually involved us playing against other Jefferson County schools that were not as racially mixed as our own. We would hear the N-word, and crowds of rival students would pepper our student buses with rocks and bricks. In my very first game playing for TJ, I scored a touchdown, and Coach saw one of the opposing players punch me as I lay on the ground in the end zone. My nose was broken, but I did not realize it and continued to play. I scored several times in that game. However, when my nose swelled up overnight, I realized it was broken.

Our team doctor, Dr. Robert Schiavone, reset it, and I was able to continue playing without missing a game.

I made the most of every opportunity I had in practice to run with the football. When we had tackling practice, I was able to demonstrate my running skills and elusiveness by making tacklers miss. It was impossible for them to tackle me one-on-one. I knew the coaches were watching closely, and I felt they were bound to put me at tailback soon, and I was right.

In my sophomore year in 1963, during one of our practice games against another school, our offense struggled to move the ball on the ground. The coaches were not happy with our performance, and I think they knew that they would have to make some changes. After that game, Coach Gray called me to his office one day before practice. He told me the coaching staff had decided to switch some players to new positions. He said they had been watching me closely and felt I would be perfect for the tailback position. He was kind of pulling my leg when he said he and the other coaches wanted to know how I felt about stepping into that position, and then he waited for my response. I am sure my facial expression gave away my feelings. Wow! I was elated and wanted to jump for joy and holler. I was so happy I could barely keep my composure. Since I didn't want to seem too excited, I just smiled and told him I would be fine with that. After I left that office, I was walking fast and grinning hard. I told myself that I would do everything within my power to make sure the coaches knew they had made the right decision.

In addition to moving me to tailback, he moved our wingback and quarterback. Coach Gray met with the team before practice and told all of us about the new changes. These changes strengthened our football team, and we were a force to be reckoned with for the remainder of my high school career.

When I got to practice and lined up at the tailback position that first day, I felt like I was on top of the world. I scored three touchdowns in my first game as a tailback, and I scored at least two in every game after that during my first year. The coaches knew they had made the right decision, and we excelled as a team from that day forward. We went the whole season, as sophomores playing a junior varsity schedule, without losing a game and without any team scoring a point against us. We had a great team, and our reputation began to spread throughout Louisville. This set the stage for the next two years of football.

Just like the basketball team at Newburg, we began to get some loyal followers from all of Newburg and other communities as well. Although most of the games in our first year were played during the day, we still had huge crowds. We became the talk of the city. Time moved on, and I developed good camaraderie with my teammates and favor with my coaches.

On occasion, some of them called me Nute, a nickname that Coach Gray had started. I'm not exactly sure where Coach Gray got that nickname from, but I have an idea. The only "Nute" I had ever heard of was the old Notre Dame football coach, Knute Rockne. Coach Rockne is credited with revolutionizing the forward pass in modern football.

During a football jamboree game at the Kentucky State Fairgrounds, Coach Gray was looking out over the field, watching us play. Suddenly, he began to yell out, correcting me and giving me a hard time. For some reason, he thought that I was not doing my job as the defensive halfback and that I was allowing the other team to gain too many yards on my side of the field. It was only a one-quarter game, and we ended in a scoreless tie.

Now, if there's one thing every football player knows, it's that when you get on that field, it doesn't matter how much you and the coach have laughed together or how well you get along. You had better perform to your maximum or else. After the game I felt bad, but only because the coach was disappointed. I knew I had done my job. I couldn't explain it to him at the time without looking as though I was making excuses, so I just let it go.

The game was filmed, and the coaches always reviewed the tapes and used them as training aids. After watching the film over the weekend, he discovered that I had done my job. We didn't win because some of my teammates were not making the right decisions and were allowing the other team to gain too much yardage. The following week, when the team met for our skull session, Coach Gray apologized to me in front of all the other players, saying, "I thought you were the one screwing up on those plays, but I was wrong. If it wasn't for you, we would have given up more yards and probably a touchdown, causing us to lose the game. You did a heck of a job, Nate, Nat, Nute, or whatever your name is."

With that, the whole locker room burst into laughter. Because it was so funny at the time, the name Nute stuck. Many of my close friends still refer to me as Nute to this very day.

The next year as juniors, we were quite a force. (By this time, TJ had added the junior year but had no senior class.) For some reason, we only played two short jamboree games and eight regular-season games during our junior year, a short schedule. Even so, and without a senior on the team, we won six games and only lost when we played the two best teams in the county, Seneca and Eastern. They were the teams that eventually played for the county championship in 1964.

I will always remember that first game against Seneca, my brother's old school. Once they had built TJ, the school board split Newburg in half, with all the Blacks living east of Newburg Road going to Seneca and those on the west side going to TJ. The split did not apply to those already at Seneca. My best friend, Will Seay, was on that Seneca team, as was Reginald Unseld, along with many of my friends and former teammates from the Broadmoor Bears, like Hilton Humphrey and Ron Garrison.

The game was at Seneca, as were all our home games, because we did not have lights on our field at that time. Both teams had been boasting all year about who would win the game. A lot was on the line, including bragging rights in Newburg for a whole year. Seneca's team was loaded with juniors and seniors, and they had too much experience and were too strong for our young players. We put up a good fight, and we gave them a real scare.

With them leading by a touchdown, we had the ball at midfield when Coach Gray called one of my favorite plays, a dive play off tackle—"dive in the five," as we called it. We lined up at the scrimmage line, and as the quarterback barked out the signals, I surveyed the Seneca team's alignment to see where the hole might be. As the quarterback took the snap and both teams sprang into motion, I started forward and took the handoff.

As our linemen met theirs, I exploded up into the hole. I made a cut to avoid their linebacker and another quick cut to elude their safety. I was off to the races for a fifty-yard touchdown run untouched. I still feel all kinds of emotions when I think of that touchdown on the same field my brother ran on.

We did not win the game, and I was as disappointed as all my teammates, coaches, classmates, teachers, and fans were. Still, I will never forget that moment when I blasted down the Seneca football field for that touchdown.

Regardless of that loss, most people would say we had a successful season. Only losing two games in our first year playing varsity football was huge, and I won the county scoring title with 18 touchdowns and 108 points while playing in only eight games. All the other teams played ten games. My teammate Ron Gathright ended up being the second-leading scorer. So although disappointed, we had a lot to be proud of in our junior year and much to look forward to in our senior year.

I was blessed to be on a terrific team with some great teammates, including Gathright, my backfield partner who played fullback. The New Orleans Saints drafted Gathright, a two-sport star at Morehead State, in 1971. Ron and I had played together since our Newburg Junior High School days. The team also included my old Newburg basketball teammates Jim DeWalt, George Lee, Billy Jackson, and Fred Johnson. Another teammate was Bob Redman, father of former Atlanta Falcons backup quarterback Chris Redman. It was an honor to play with these guys. They, along with many others, helped to make me the person that I am and the player that I became. On the field, they opened holes in the defense that allowed me to gain the yards and score the touchdowns that gave me the reputation that I achieved.

I have to give these guys credit. The privilege of playing with them, combined with other key factors, such as the time and place I grew up in and my family, coaches, and supporters, really got me ready for some football.

My senior year, we were favored to win both the football and basketball championships because of our veteran teams—which now had seniors for the first time. It looked as though I would be heading toward another scoring title. We won the first three games, and then I had a bad break, literally. I broke my hand in the third game and had to miss the next three games. I don't know when the break occurred, but I should have known something was wrong when I fumbled the ball a couple of times. I continued to play with the pain and did not discover the break until the next day when I woke up with a swollen hand.

With Gathright taking over my tailback slot and some excellent backup runners like Jimmy Hudson, Wilbur Hudson, and Artis Seay filling in, we were able to win those three games that I missed. It was agonizing to sit on the sidelines, unable to play the game I loved so much. I couldn't wait until the hand healed. I returned to action halfway through the season and picked up where I had left off before the injury, scoring four touchdowns in my first game back. I had lost too much ground to win another scoring title, but the most important thing was to stay undefeated and win the championship. TJ did retain the county scoring title, however, with Gathright earning that honor.

We were undefeated going into the county championship game against our archrival, Seneca High School. The Redskins from Seneca had lost one game, so if our game with them ended in a tie, we would win the county championship, and then we'd play the city champions for the AAA title. We were ready to avenge the previous year's loss to them, and we knew we had the most talent and the best team. We had no doubts we would win the game and the title. There was simply no way we would lose. N-O, no way!

The night of the game, the crowd was absolutely standing room only. If that stadium could have held thirty thousand, I believe we could have filled it up. Not only was all of Newburg there, including Dad, who never missed a game, but so were all the Seneca faithful. I'm sure all the media outlets and a slew of college scouts were there as well. Both teams were loaded with talented college prospects, and many went on to play at the college level.

We were as ready as we could be. But Gathright had been nursing a bad ankle for several games. As fate would have it, his ankle flared up, and he was only about 80 percent up to par. Against an outstanding Seneca team, we knew that might be too much to overcome. This would be my final game on the Seneca field, where I had scored numerous touchdowns for TJ. It was now showtime, and the game was a total defensive battle. It seemed like they knew every play we would run before we ran it. We both fought gamely, but they took the lead with a touchdown and an extra point to make it 7-0 going into the last quarter.

The game was well into the second half when I finally broke loose for a fourth-quarter touchdown to pull within one point of a tie score. It was nothing spectacular, but we were just happy to get on the scoreboard at last. Gathright was our extra-point kicker, and he was accurate. He could really boom them through, high above the goal posts, but the referees used that asset against us. He kicked the ball, and it appeared to be good, but because his kick was so high and the goal posts so low, the referees called it wide. We could not believe they had made that call, and there were no instant replays to look at.

All we needed was a tie, and we would be playing for the AAA championship. The coaches protested vehemently, to no avail. The refs would not reverse the call, and we lost the game and a chance for the championship. What a way to lose the game for which we had waited so long and worked so hard.

We were completely devastated, but we had no reason to be ashamed. We had given it all we had, but the other side had pulled out the win. Our friends on the Seneca team consoled us, and we congratulated them on a great game. And besides, if you lose a game, who better to lose to than some of your best friends? We had an outstanding season with a 9–1 win-loss record, and Gathright and I made the All-State team again. It took many years for me and my friends at TJ to be at peace with that game. In football, as in life, things don't always go your way, but you have to remember that the sun will shine in the morning. You have to get up and keep going.

Thomas Jefferson High School would have to wait several years before it finally won the title. When it won the AAA championship in 1971, two of the members of that team were my brothers Kenneth and Michael Northington. Michael was an All-State and All-American player. He went on to become a star running back and defensive back at Purdue University and was drafted by the Washington Redskins (now the Commanders). For a long time, he was tied for the Big Ten record for most touchdowns in a game, five. In track, Kenneth was the state champion in the 100- and 220-yard dash, and he helped TJ win the state track championship, dethroning perennial champion Male High School. He went on to play football at the University of Kentucky and was on the team that won the Peach Bowl in 1976. Kenneth was the high school track coach of Lexington, Kentucky, native Tyson Gay, Olympic athlete and American record holder in the 100-meter dash. Other stars on my brothers' AAA championship football team included Ben Thomas and Ray Carr, both of whom followed in my footsteps to UK.

I believe God gave the Northington family its share of athletic talent. Each member of my family was gifted. Our entire family enjoyed sports and athleticism, and many times, we enjoyed them together. Both my parents said they could run very fast, and I can believe that because my brothers and sisters and I can run fast. I truly believe that if my two older brothers or my sisters had competed in track, they would have excelled at that too and won some titles.

After the loss to Seneca, we did not have a lot of time to feel sorry for ourselves. Basketball practice would start the next week, and we were touted as one of the best teams in the state. Oh, by the way, we never lost to Seneca in basketball the two years we played them. We had an outstanding basketball team, with essentially the same starters as on our football team. I played guard along with Gale Daniels, with Gathright and Redman at forward positions and DeWalt at the center. One of our backup forwards was future University of Louisville and Kentucky Colonels forward Ron Thomas, an underclassman who came on strong at the end of the year. Robert Unseld was another underclassman who was instrumental in our going to the state championship. We had some great talent. We had a great senior season, as expected, winning the sixth regional championship against our former junior high school coach, Robert Graves, and his Central High School team.

That was the first year the Louisville schools were divided into two regions: the sixth and seventh. The game was at the Freedom Hall Arena, home of the University of Louisville, with a full house of eighteen thousand people. The fans saw two great games that night, with the Male High Bulldogs defeating Westport High for the seventh region title. We had a tough game going down to the final buzzer, but we squeaked out a bittersweet win against our old coach. This win meant that in the very first year of having a senior class, TJ won the sixth region championship and was going to the Kentucky state championship, "the Sweet Sixteen," as it is called. The students, faculty, and all our community supporters were thrilled, and of course the team was as well.

The state tournament was also held at Freedom Hall, which was one of the largest basketball arenas in the country in 1966. Freedom Hall hosted six of the NCAA Men's Final Four College Basketball Championships, 1958, 1959, 1962, 1963, 1967, and 1969, when the University of California at Los Angeles had those great teams. The state basketball tournament in Kentucky is second only to the NCAA Tournament. Other activities in the state essentially shut down for a week as the sixteen teams come from every region. Kentucky is a basketball state and usually has great talent every year. The talent has fallen off over the last few years, but at one time, it was second to none.

All our fans from Newburg and TJ were excited, getting out of school for a week to go to the tournament. Basketball is king in Kentucky, and the TJ Patriots were the toast of Louisville, along with the Male Bulldogs.

The state tournament started the week after the regional championship, and we played great, winning our first two games to make it to the semifinals, or the Final Four. Our semifinal game was scheduled first that morning against an outstanding Shelby County team led by future UK star Mike Casey. These guys were good and could shoot the lights out, so we knew we were in for a real dogfight.

The game started, and during the first quarter, our leading scorer and rebounder and our best player, Ron Gathright, was called for two quick fouls. With his effectiveness reduced, we were taken out of our game, and were not able to be as aggressive defensively as we normally would. We liked to press and put on the pressure. Now, with the game being called so closely, we had to sit back, and they shot the ball too well for that. We lost a close game to Shelby County, and they beat Male that night to win the state championship.

With our loss, we had suffered another disappointment, but I guess God had some lessons for us to learn that year. It is true that adversity makes you stronger, and we definitely were growing tougher from the lessons we were learning playing football and basketball. Naturally, in those days, everybody wanted to be state champions, and we had come very close in both football and basketball. Even though we came up short, not many athletes could say they accomplished as much as we did in our high school careers. Regardless of how the scores came out, we were champions.

The community and all our fans were naturally disappointed, but we knew they were proud of what our players and coaches at TJ had accomplished in only three short years of existence. They were proud of us, and we were proud of how they supported us and stood by us. That is real love. We laid the foundation for the young men who would follow in our footsteps. I am sure many young boys who watched us perform had the same feeling I had had when I saw my older brother play for Seneca. My younger brothers and my nephew, Courtney Montgomery, were watching, and they all became stars at TJ as well. Courtney was the smart one; he stuck with basketball, but he had the speed and talent to star in football if he had chosen to do so.

Many of the young onlookers went on to break our records and make a name for themselves because of the examples we had set as student athletes. Among them were Ron Thomas (University of Louisville and ABA star with the Kentucky Colonels); Ben Thomas (UK); my brothers Mike Northington (Purdue) and Ken Northington (UK); Tony Gray (UK); Elmore Stephens (UK All-SEC tight end); Cecil Bowen (UK); Ray Carr (UK); Carey Eaves (UK); and Charles Mitchell (Eastern Kentucky University), just to name a few.

We all made our mark on the sports world in different ways. Despite the obvious obstacles for Blacks back then, we were determined that nothing would stop us from showing our faces on the fields, courts, tracks, and diamonds of the American sports world.

Unfortunately, I am sad to say that in the 1980s, the Jefferson County School Board disregarded all this sports history and school spirit and closed the high school, turning it back into a middle school. In spite of that, the sports records, the teachers, the fans, the students, and the memories will live on.

Geographically, the school was right on the fringe of the Black Newburg community, and the board of education cited integration and busing as reasons to close the high school. It allowed schools in other communities with less seniority than TJ to continue existing as they were. While there were probably many reasons for their decision, I believe the location of the school and the success of its athletic programs, especially football, basketball, and track, were possible factors. However, life must go on, and I am grateful for the experiences God provided for me there.

I want to give special thanks to everyone who had a part in making TJ the school it was: the teachers, the students, the parents, the boosters, and the supporters not only from Newburg but from throughout the city of Louisville. I am thankful and blessed that my experience at TJ left me with so many good memories and so many wonderful friends.

One of those memories was meeting and getting to know my future wife, the mother of my wonderful children. During my senior year, I met Dollye Bowman, who actually lived only four blocks down the street from my house in the Newburg neighborhood and who was in her first year at TJ. I had noticed this cute little girl walking home from Newburg School or from the store on numerous occasions, but by the time she started attending high school at TJ, she had grown up to be a very pretty young lady.

After she became a member of the drill team, I began to see her around more—either at practice after school or before or after the football games. Because of my busy football schedule and because I was a little shy as well, I never got up the nerve to ask her for her phone number or ask her out to a movie. But she was a little more outgoing than me, and as I was heading to my locker on the second floor one day, she walked up to me and said, "When you get your senior pictures back, would you give me one?"

I replied that I would, but more importantly, I decided I was not going to let that opportunity pass without asking for a date, and so our relationship began.

She was a smart, intelligent, gentle, and loving person who liked to laugh, and she loved sports as well. We dated for the remainder of my senior year and continued when I went to UK for two years, finally marrying after I left UK. Dollye was a wonderful young Christian woman, and later she became a devoted wife and mother. I owe a lot to her for her love and devotion throughout our years of marriage. Unfortunately, our marriage did not last, and that is regrettable; however, God blessed us with two beautiful children, six grandchildren, and two great-grandchildren. I can truly say the breakup was not due to any failure on her part, and I accept full responsibility. I regret that I was not the same person during that time that I am today. In life, we have to face some undesirable consequences of our actions, but we must learn and benefit from those failures.

I am happy that when we repent and confess our faults God is faithful and just forgives us and gives us a second chance. He blessed me with a second chance by giving me another loving, God-fearing wife who has been very inspirational and supportive in my life.

But I am getting ahead of myself. Before I get to that chapter in my life, I need to get to my time at UK and my experience of playing some football.

6

Game On

Freshman Football

The very first college that showed interest in me as a football prospect was Purdue University in West Lafayette, Indiana. In the 1960s, Purdue had one of the best football teams in the Big Ten Conference, plus a Hall of Fame coach, Jack Mollenkopf. In 1965, when I was a senior in high school, my football coach, Jim Gray, who is also in the Kentucky Athletic Hall of Fame, informed me that the Purdue University football coaches had contacted him through Robert Holloway, a local Purdue alumnus. They wanted to know if I would be interested in making an official visit to the school and attending a football game. I didn't know much about Purdue at the time, although I had seen them play on television. I had heard more about Ohio State, Michigan, Michigan State, and other members of the Big Ten Conference. However, I was thrilled that a college from the Big Ten was interested in me, so I told him I was interested.

Mr. Holloway had seen me play against his nephew, who was a quarterback on another local team. I had had two good games against that team and had made quite an impression.

When I attended the Purdue game, I was very impressed with the whole college atmosphere. People were coming into this small college town from all over the region to attend the ball game against Miami University of Ohio. This was my first experience with fans tailgating before a football game, and I found it exciting. This was "big-time" football. The stadium was a huge bowl with a seating capacity of more than sixty thousand. Since I had never attended a college football game in person before, just being in that atmosphere had me spellbound. You can see a college game on television, but you can't get the real feel of the game unless you see it in person. It was unbelievable.

In addition to the big stadium and field house, Purdue had a new basketball arena (Mackey Arena) under construction right next to the stadium. These athletic facilities were quite impressive, especially to a young teenager from a small neighborhood like Newburg. The fans' enthusiasm was unmatched by anything I had seen at a sporting event. There were the cheerleaders, the marching band, and the drill team, and flags with the school colors were waving everywhere. They had a students' section, and all the fans seemed to be hyped to the max. The atmosphere was electric. This was college football at its best.

The coach of the Miami of Ohio team at that time was Bo Schembechler, who went on to become a College Football Hall of Fame coach at the University of Michigan. The quarterback of that Purdue football team was none other than Robert Allen "Bob" Griese, who would eventually become an NFL Hall of Fame quarterback. He won three consecutive Super Bowl games with the Miami Dolphins. Griese was almost a one-man team that day. He was the quarterback, punter, and placekicker. About the only thing he didn't do was lead cheers, and I believe I saw him doing that once. I had never seen anything like that before, and I was highly impressed with his skills.

I also had a great basketball player, Herm Gilliam, show me around the campus. If that name sounds familiar, it should. Gilliam, from Winston-Salem, North Carolina, was a number-one draft choice by the Cincinnati Royals who later played with the Portland Trail Blazers, who won the NBA championship in 1977. Gilliam passed away in 2005. I will remember him as a very articulate, friendly young man. I guess I must have been high on the coaches' radar for them to put me in such company as that.

I could see myself playing football in that arena. At six feet and 175 pounds (I bulked up to 195 my senior year in college), I knew I didn't have great size, like some of the halfbacks in the Big Ten, but with my speed and athletic ability, I was confident I could be a star in that league. Mr. Holloway explained that the coaches were not concerned because they did not want to miss signing another small running back from Louisville, as they had in 1961 when they had an opportunity to get Sherman Lewis, an All-State football player and track star from Louisville duPont Manual High School. Lewis went on to become an All-American football player at Michigan State University. Yes, this was the same Sherman Lewis I had seen blazing around the bases playing softball at Newburg Park when I was a young teen. If they had asked me, I could have told them his small stature did not matter. The Purdue coaches had decided he was too small (about five feet, nine inches and 165 pounds) for major college football and did not recruit him, but after playing against him at Michigan State for three years, they realized they had made a terrible mistake. Sherman Lewis was the fourth-highest vote getter for the Heisman Trophy in 1964. I was honored they felt I had the kind of talent and skill to be compared to a star like Sherman Lewis.

The Purdue team had a great game that day, winning against a feisty but outclassed Miami of Ohio team. After the game, I was invited to the locker room to meet some of the players. Later I met with Coach Mollenkopf and some of the other coaches. They told me they were willing to offer me a scholarship to become a Purdue Boilermaker and asked when I would be making my decision about accepting a football scholarship. I told them I would make a decision after my basketball season was over. Mr. Holloway was happy that the coaches wanted me to attend Purdue, and we discussed the pros and cons all the way back to Louisville. I told him that I had really enjoyed the game and loved the atmosphere and that I would more than likely decide to become a Boilermaker.

I never had another opportunity to speak with any of the Purdue coaches again. Although I did not accept a scholarship to play for Purdue, my brother Michael, a high school All-American football player at TJ, accepted a scholarship in 1972 and became an outstanding player for the Boilermakers, scoring five touchdowns in one game to tie the Big Ten record. The same gentleman who had sought to recruit me in 1965, Robert Holloway, recruited Michael, who was later drafted by the Washington Redskins of the NFL. He also recruited my brother Kenneth out of high school. The last time I saw Mr. Holloway was at Dad's wake. He reminded me of the great opportunity I missed out on by not becoming a Purdue Boilermaker.

I am honored he still remembered the ability I had after all those years. Mr. Holloway didn't do so badly in his recruiting efforts for his alma mater.

He was able to get one outstanding Northington football player out of three. Going 1-for-3 at the plate in baseball will make you a Hall of Famer. He remained a true friend to Michael and the Northington family throughout the years, which spoke volumes for his character, and he was a Hall of Famer.

Since I chose to break the color barrier in the SEC, I was not with the Purdue football team in 1967 when they became champions of the Big Ten Conference. It would have been nice to play with Purdue in the Rose Bowl on New Year's Day in 1968, but God has plans for us that ultimately make us the champions he wants us to be. Hindsight enables me to live at peace with my decisions. I put thoughts of Purdue behind me and moved on.

It was August 1966 when I arrived at UK for my freshman year, and if you think Blacks were scarce on campus, you should have seen the football locker room. When UK was recruiting me, I had asked how many Blacks were enrolled in the school, and someone had told me "several thousand." They could have said "several hundred," and even that might have been an exaggeration. But I guess the desire to have me come to UK might have caused them to stretch the truth just a little. Regardless, I was happy to be there, and while I had never allowed race or other people's reactions to my skin color to discourage me from anything, I felt that a little more color on the team couldn't hurt. Enter Greg Page.

He was born in 1948 and grew up in Middlesboro, Kentucky (sometimes spelled Middlesborough). The town was located in Bell County, about 150 miles southeast of Louisville. When we reported to UK to begin our first year, the powers that be decided, as you might expect, that Greg and I should be roommates, along with two white freshmen, Phil Thompson from Louisville and Marty New from Hamilton, Ohio, in a dorm designated for the freshman football team. Phil and Marty were good, friendly roommates and were two real cutups who were always joking around and keeping things lively. We did not have any problems whatsoever, and we all got along well as roommates, teammates, and friends.

In retrospect, I believe the coaches' choice of those two as our roommates was a strategic move, because Phil and Marty were accustomed to playing on teams with Blacks. Phil was a high school All-American from Seneca who had caught the winning touchdown pass against TJ my senior year. He became one of our best friends on the UK team. His brother worked with me, and after many years, Phil and I began communicating on the internet. He experienced some tough health issues, but his faith was strong, and my prayers were always with him.

Since the Kentucky athletic program's nickname was the Wildcats, the varsity team's dorm was dubbed Wildcat Manor. The freshman dorm was located right next door to Wildcat Manor. Unfortunately, Kitten Lodge, the name of our living quarters, wasn't as cool.

Off the football field, the athletes at UK received first-class treatment. I think some of us might have felt that the basketball team was treated more like royalty. If so, that might have had a little something to do with its four national NCAA titles. With a record like that, I would say they deserved it. The UK football team, on the other hand, was always struggling to be among the elite teams of the SEC and the nation, although they had won a championship in the 1950s, under the legendary football coach Paul "Bear" Bryant. The university administration, alumni, and boosters had a strong desire to do whatever it took to elevate the football program and realized one of the best ways to compete for the top talent was to have outstanding training and game facilities. There was no question the school administrators and boosters were totally committed to providing the football program with the very best facilities they possibly could.

I thought every school was equipped as well as UK was, but that was not the case, as I would later discover. Our football practice facility was excellent, and the treatment was too. The equipment manager gave us freshly laundered, clean practice gear every day. The practice area included several fields with a twenty-five- or thirty-foot tower for the head coach to oversee the entire complex.

Coach Bradshaw would often stand on the tower with his bullhorn and angrily shout out directions and commands during practice. Occasionally he would give out some praise, but that was rare. The upperclassmen said he had mellowed some over the years, especially since there had been an investigation into the brutality of the practices several years prior and the program had been placed on a one-year probation. This, by the way, was unknown to my parents and me when we agreed to accept the scholarship. I don't know if that would have made a difference. You can always accuse a coach of being too tough, but the fact is that football is a tough sport.

In the freshman dorm at UK, we had our own cafeteria and cooks, as well as separate recreation and study rooms. The southern cooks (including several Blacks) really knew how to make the food taste almost as if it were homemade. I say almost because nobody could cook like my mother. We could not help but gain weight because we were encouraged to eat all we could. Since we were big, healthy football players, we didn't need any extra encouragement. Twice a week (Tuesdays and Thursdays) during the football season, we had T-bone steak, sweet tea, baked potatoes, and all the usual trimmings that went with a first-class meal like that. I don't care who you are or where you're from, that's what I call royal treatment.

On one weekend, I returned to the dorm late, after the dining room closed, to find some of my teammates in the kitchen cooking up a feast. I mean they were cooking everything. I didn't know what to think; it seemed harmless enough at the time, and besides, I was hungry, so I joined in. I found out someone had taken the window out of the door and cut out the nails to make it appear to be intact, and after the dining room closed, they simply removed the window and started cooking. Unfortunately, and as always, the coaches learned of this and put a stop to it. We had to do some extra running as punishment. Hey, boys will be boys.

When we reported to fall practice about a week before the other students arrived, there was naturally an atmosphere of great anticipation from the news media, as well as football supporters, coaches, and our teammates. This was the first time in the history of Kentucky football and the SEC that Black players were on scholarship to play football.

Of course, thousands of freshman and varsity players were reporting to fall camp at hundreds of schools across the country around this time, but my mind was not on those; UK was my prime concern. Thirty freshmen reported to training camp from many different states, both near and far. The majority were from Kentucky, of course, but there were young men from Florida, Ohio, Pennsylvania, Tennessee, South Carolina, New Jersey, and even as far away as New Mexico. We all came with the same excitement and anticipation of playing major college football in one of the most dominant leagues in the country. As young adults, we were still a little inexperienced and naive, but there was no way any of us could have known at the time that of the thirty freshmen who had reported to UK for football and a college education that year, only nine would stay around for the next four years. It is not unusual for several football players to quit the team over the course of several years, but to have such a high number leave is unthinkable.

Playing football is tough work, and fall camp is beyond the average person's imagination. Now, add to that the fact that all eyes were on Greg Page and me, and you get an idea of the pressure we faced. However, I had spent the summer in Lexington working for a brick mason and had played in the East-West All-Star game a few weeks before football camp began, so I had had an opportunity to become familiar with the city and the campus. Greg and I had met the week of the All-Star game, and we naturally hit it off right away.

While we were in Lexington for the All-Star game in August 1966, a reporter interviewed Greg and me, along with some of the coaches, students, and fans, for an Associated Press article. It quoted us as saying we were giving less thought to integration than to our abilities on the football field. We conceded that we were nervous but said that our anxiety had more to do with football than integration. I said that everybody was nervous the first few days but that I was sure things would be fine after we got more comfortable being together. Greg added, "Yeah, you are among strangers, and it takes a little while to get to know each other."

One of the fans stated he was less concerned about the color of the players and more about their football talent. I was happy to see that at least some of the UK fans were supportive of our position, and I prayed that there would be thousands more who felt the same way. Up to that point, there had been no reason to feel otherwise. Only time would tell.

That same article reported that Vanderbilt University had signed Perry Wallace to become the first African American basketball player on scholarship in the SEC. The Associated Press said that other schools were scouting Blacks as well. Integration had come to the SEC.

In 1966, the NCAA rules did not permit freshman football players in Division I (major colleges) to participate in varsity games—although we were given some leeway to practice with the varsity team on a limited basis. So the majority of our practices would be restricted to the freshman players, and we even had our own schedule of four freshman games. Our first game would be against our archrival, the University of Tennessee, and the others were against Virginia Tech, Cincinnati, and Vanderbilt. Once we had received our locker assignments and picked up our practice gear, we joyfully hit the practice field with great anticipation. Of course, all eyes were on Greg Page and me.

Greg was an outstanding football player, like many of the young men in our freshman class. He was a high school All-Stater, and the coaches expected him to be a starter at UK and one of the top defensive ends in the SEC for many years to come. They felt that his potential was unlimited. As a defensive lineman, Greg was taller and weighed more than me, standing about six feet, two inches tall and weighing about 215 pounds. That was a good size for a freshman lineman, and he was strong and powerful. He had a great sense of humor, and if Greg Page was around, you could always count on an upbeat atmosphere and a good laugh at just the right time. One of the things I admired most about my friend was that he seemed to be color-blind. Greg could find the good in anything. He usually laughed off incidents that would have hurt, angered, or offended most other people. He loved his family and often spoke highly of them. For many reasons that go beyond the color of our skin, Greg became the best friend I could ever have had in college. It's a blessing he was my roommate.

Greg reminded me of my best friend, Will Seay. They were similar in build and personality. Both were fun-loving, outgoing, and personable young men who could get along with just about anyone. They were true gentle giants, big in stature but possessing big hearts as well. They enjoyed life and treated everyone with dignity and respect. Neither would do anything to hurt anyone in any way. I feel God put Greg in my life the same way he had done with Will.

My personality was different from theirs. I was quieter and a little more reserved, but that's the way most of my siblings were. I like to think of myself as a friendly person who gets along well with just about anyone. I believe in the Golden Rule and believe in treating everyone with respect. I have many lifelong friends. I will admit that, unlike Greg, I need some time to get close to others. But our personalities were compatible, and we became excellent friends.

On and off the field, Greg and I would banter. Whenever I intercepted a pass during scrimmages or ran back a punt return for a touchdown during intrasquad games, Greg would say, "Man, you sure are lucky! How did you do that?"

Of course, he knew I would always have a response to things like that. Usually I would just smile and say, "You know that's not luck. I can do that because I'm just good."

We understood each other, and he knew my ability, so I knew he really was teasing. These days when I watch the SEC games on television during the football season, seeing all the African American players for Tennessee, Alabama, Florida, Louisiana, Georgia, Mississippi, and the other schools in the conference, I get a sense of amazement that Greg and I were the first at Kentucky and in the SEC. It is hard to believe that the league has come so far. At times it may not be clear, but America really has come a long way. I wish that UK would do more to honor the historical contributions made by Greg Page and me. I believe that an effort should be made to let every incoming freshman know the roles we played in integrating the athletic program at UK and the SEC. I believe our breaking down the barrier of segregation was monumental in healing many wounds and in allowing people of different racial, social, economic, and cultural backgrounds to come together for a common cause. What we accomplished is unfathomable.

Even while I was writing this book, a coworker told me she had recently seen a poster of me at the Kentucky football training facility at Nutter Field House, and on another occasion, a coworker heard a television announcer talk about me being the first to integrate the league as they showed a picture of me. I have heard comments from many people over the course of time. It might seem that I should have the proverbial big head, but I am grateful that God allows me to take it all in stride and realize that I could not have done anything if not for his will. He is the one who made it all possible, and I can always say, "To God be the glory."

After weeks of hard practices and competition for positions, we were anxious to see some actual game action. In high school, we would have had a game by that time of the year, so we had grown weary of practicing without a game. It seemed as if it would never arrive, but the time finally came for our very first freshman game. With only thirty players on the freshman team, and with some of those out with injuries, we knew everyone would see playing time, but of course all competitive athletes want to play the position they like the best. I had prepared for both the offensive tailback and defensive cornerback positions, but of course my preference was the tailback. Our first game was going to be against the University of Tennessee (UT) in Knoxville. A natural rivalry existed between our teams, most likely because they are neighbors.

Historically, UT has dominated Kentucky in football much the same way that Kentucky has dominated Tennessee in basketball. Freshman games did not officially count for the record books, but because of the rivalry, it felt as though all games against Tennessee meant a lot.

We felt that this game was just as important as a varsity football game. I believe the varsity players also wanted us to come home with a victory. The three-hour drive down Interstate 75 from Lexington to Knoxville is a beautiful one as you ascend the foothills of the Appalachian Mountains. We couldn't even enjoy the scenery, however, because our minds were set on the ball game. As UK freshmen, this was our first opportunity to show our coaches what we could do in a game, and we were eager to make a good impression on them and on the other team. We were pumped up.

As we turned a corner and got our first glimpse of the Tennessee football stadium, every player on the bus became about as quiet as a church mouse. That was the largest football stadium most of us had ever seen. It was something to behold. Our stadium back home at UK (Stoll Field/McLean Stadium) had a seating capacity of only thirty-seven thousand, but Neyland Stadium could comfortably seat more than fifty thousand. It is the largest stadium in the SEC and the sixth largest in the world. From a player's perspective, it was a little intimidating. As things turned out, we wouldn't have to contend with hordes of rabid fans because only a small crowd showed up to watch. It was only a freshman football game, held on a weekday, when students were either studying or doing other things. When game time came, none of that discouraged us. Our only concern was that we were playing against such an archrival. Simply having the opportunity to play in that kind of atmosphere on that field was thrilling and rewarding.

As we suited up in the Kentucky blue uniform and ran onto the field for our very first game, we felt tremendous pride and satisfaction. That day we were no longer high school athletes but official college players. We wanted to put everything on the line, show what we were made of, and come out with a victory.

When the coach gave us the starting lineup, I was disappointed that I would not get to start on offense, but I was starting as a defensive back and as a kickoff returner. I thought that during our preseason practices I had been as impressive as any of the other tailbacks, but I also knew that eventually my time would come.

In high school, I had easily landed a starting position, but at UK, the competition was tough. We had a large number of excellent players at the tailback position, including Roger Gann, who was a high school All-American out of North Carolina. Everyone wants to start, but only so many positions are available, so I knew I would just have to keep working hard and wait until the coaches gave me a shot. My opportunity would come, and when it did, I would get out there and make it count. I understood, but still I was not happy. I waited my turn, and sure enough, it didn't take long for me to get my first taste of action.

After Tennessee scored, I went in to return a kickoff. I was a little nervous as I got into position to field the kick, but I had done this too many times to count, first in sandlot and then in high school, so I was ready. The referee blew the whistle, and the kicker kicked the ball. It was a high end-over-end kick, and I moved into position to field it, keeping my eyes fixed on the ball as I saw my teammates retreating into position to block for me. I fielded the ball cleanly, took off as fast as I could, and immediately scanned the field looking for openings. With Tennessee's defenders closing in on me, I got some terrific blocks. Then I spotted an inviting gap up the middle, and I burst through. It looked as if I might have a lane to go all the way.

Eluding tacklers and cutting toward the sidelines, I covered thirty-two yards before I was finally brought down. I thought, "Man, I almost went all the way." We had good field position to start our series. I really wanted a chance to run with the football on offense, but I played most of the game as a defensive back. It was a hard-fought game, and although we played excellently, we lost by a touchdown, 21–14. One of my teammates returned a punt for a touchdown, but it was called back because of a penalty. That play proved to be the deciding factor in the game's final outcome. We made a good showing, and I believe the coaches were satisfied with our performance overall.

I made a couple of good kickoff returns and was satisfied with my performance in my first college action, but I was more determined than ever to win the starting tailback position. I knew it would not be easy because we had some outstanding tailbacks. I definitely had my work cut out for me.

Greg had a big game, making several big tackles and putting a lot of pressure on the quarterback from his defensive-end position. We both felt good about being part of the team and earning the confidence of our coaches and teammates. We had just experienced the joy and thrill of college football, even though it had only been at the freshman level. We always felt like we were an integral part of the UK football program, and it had been a team effort—not Black or white, but team—together. Nobody said it, but I believe everyone accepted Greg and me a little bit more that day. There is nothing like pulling together as teammates and having one another's backs to make you forget about the color of someone's skin.

If there were any questions about whether Greg or I could play, they were answered on that Tennessee football field that day. Of course, because of the rivalry with UT, we were disappointed about this loss, but that would be the only freshman game we would lose all season, and the loss just made us more determined to work harder and be more focused.

7

"That's How You Do It!"

My next game as a freshman was against Virginia Tech. It was an away game as well, but this time, instead of driving, we flew into Blacksburg, Virginia, the day before the game. I was just a young country boy from Kentucky, and here I was, sitting on a huge jet plane for the first time. At first, some of the players, including me, were apprehensive about flying. Back then, not many of us had traveled very much or very far from home. In the beginning, I held on tight to the armrests, laid my head back, and, of course, prayed a bit. I'll never forget the feeling in my stomach when the plane dropped a little from the turbulence or the cottony look of the clouds as they slowly moved under the plane.

I paid attention to every sound the airplane made and looked around to see how the experienced travelers were reacting. I noticed that the flight staff and coaches didn't seem worried at all. Seeing their confidence gave me confidence as well. It helped that the flight attendants were friendly, attentive, and, unlike today, generous with the peanuts. After a while I was okay, and the flight wasn't very long. I don't know what I had expected, but things went smoothly.

Once we arrived, we had a little walk-through practice, and after dinner we went to a movie before returning to our hotel. I had gotten more chances to work with the offensive team in practice, so I thought the coaches would use me on offense and not just on defense as in the Tennessee game. The coach had let us know that he was not completely satisfied with our running game, and I thought that maybe he wanted a little more speed in our backfield. The tailbacks and fullbacks had done a good job against UT, but sometimes it doesn't hurt to change things up and throw another wrinkle at the defense. One of our staple plays was the tailback end sweep, and it helps to have a quick, speedy tailback that can either take it wide and get the edge or find a crease and cut it up. I was ready to be that man. Even if I didn't start at tailback, I felt they would play me at some point during the game and I would be ready. The next day, when it was time to play, just as I had thought, I was not the starter with the offensive squad, but just as in the first game, I was the number-one player returning kickoffs that day.

In the beginning, our team struggled to move the ball. Normally, Duke Owen, our freshman coach, was an upbeat and animated kind of person, very excitable. When he saw we were unable to move the ball effectively down the field, he quickly became quite agitated and visibly disappointed. We started the second quarter, and after another run went for little or no yardage, the coach became even more upset. He was tired of seeing our team going nowhere. Things were not looking good, and I could only imagine what would happen at halftime in the locker room.

After coming off the field after a defensive series, I was standing on the sidelines just watching the game and hoping my teammates could make it happen, when suddenly the coach turned and waved for me to come forward. I was eager, and I ran up to him quickly—but not quickly enough for the coach, I guess. He angrily yelled, "Get in there!" As I ran onto the field, I was nervous but excited, thinking, "Now this is my chance. This is my chance!"

As we huddled, the quarterback called a tailback sweep, and I was to be the ball carrier. This had been one of my favorite plays in high school, one I had run hundreds of times since I was a kid. I particularly liked that play because it gave me the opportunity to use my speed and quickness to run around the end of the line, instead of up the middle, with two or three big blockers leading the way. The huddle broke, and everyone lined up in their positions. I was directly behind the quarterback, with my feet spread and both hands on my knees. As he called the signals, I visualized how I was going to run and what I was going to do, just as my old high school coach had taught me.

As the center snapped the ball, everyone went into motion. I took a quick step to my left, raising my hands into position to take the pitch from the quarterback. He took the snap and turned to pitch me the ball. As I caught it, I was in the second or third step and heading toward the sideline. I remembered Dad telling me to watch my blockers, and that's exactly what I did. I saw my blockers form and patiently waited for the play to develop so I could make my cut toward the goal line. I was going about three-quarter speed as I watched the play develop. I knew that timing was crucial.

Suddenly I saw a hole. At just the right time I planted my foot, cut back against the grain, and exploded through the hole, as I had done numerous times. I eluded the first wave of defenders, and out of the corner of my eye, I saw others coming up to tackle me, but I juked one of them and sidestepped another. As I cleared the last defender, I turned on the speed, burst into the open, and headed toward the goal line. I sprinted forty-three yards, outrunning all the remaining defenders for the touchdown!

That was my first run from scrimmage and my first touchdown in college. I felt as though I had scored the winning touchdown for the NFL championship. My teammates ran to meet and congratulate me, with Greg leading the way as I turned and headed toward the sidelines. I saw our coach jumping up and down. I trotted back over to the team, and the coach patted me on the back. He turned to the other players, loudly shouting, "Now that's how you do it! That's how you do it!"

That touchdown seemed to be the catalyst that we needed to get on track to play a good game. We beat Virginia Tech 37–8 that day. Because we won, I must have forgotten to be scared on the flight back to Lexington. I was happy to finally get a chance to play offense, run with the ball, and score a touchdown. After that, I became the starting tailback, and I really appreciated the coaches giving me that opportunity.

Just as he did against Tennessee, Greg had a good game as well, sacking the quarterback and making several tackles for losses. We were gaining respect and had begun making names for ourselves.

The varsity coaches and players greeted us warmly after our victory over Virginia Tech. It really felt good having a victory under our belts, and we had a great practice week in preparation for our first home game, against the University of Cincinnati. This would be the first opportunity for the Kentucky fans, students, and our families to come out to see us play. By game day, October 20, 1966, we couldn't wait to hit the field in our Big Blue uniforms in front of our own fans.

Even my old high school coach, Jim Gray, drove the seventy-seven miles from Louisville to see me play in this game. So did my parents, of course. Dad would not be able to walk up and down the sidelines as he did during high school games, but I knew he would be up there in the stands, and Greg's family would be there as well.

Although this was just a freshman game, it would be the first time two African Americans would play a football game on Stoll Field for UK. It would not be the history-making event that playing varsity in the SEC would be, but it was definitely a first. I felt good as Greg and I ran onto that field to begin our warm-up. We received a warm reception that made us feel even better. It was strange, but I did not feel nervous. In fact, I felt very relaxed.

Once the game started, it didn't take long for us to give our fans something to cheer about. I dropped back to our ten-yard line to receive the opening kickoff. I jumped up and down to stay loose as the teams lined up. My mind was working overtime visualizing how I would catch the ball and execute the play. I knew that with a couple of good blocks and some quick cuts I could take the pigskin all the way for an opening touchdown. I could even visualize the crowd cheering as I sprinted down the sideline for a hundred-yard touchdown. Then the referee blew the whistle, and the kicker approached the ball and gave it a tremendous boot. The game was on. As the kick came high and tumbling, I watched it drop into my arms. I immediately sprinted up the field searching for a lane to run through as my teammates made some dynamite blocks on the Cincinnati defenders. I saw an opening to my left and made a quick cut, avoiding a tackler and leaving him reaching for air. I turned on the speed as I faked out another tackler. Just as it looked as if I would break into the open, one of the men I had faked recovered and grabbed my ankle. I fell down to the turf as the fans first gave a sigh and then cheered and applauded the dazzling run. I had come so close to breaking free for a touchdown, and I couldn't believe

I had let that guy tackle me. I should have been able to keep my balance without going down so easily, but I had a great day, and we won the game.

Although I did not score a touchdown, the yardage I gained running the ball helped contribute to our victory. Our defense was stellar, with Greg having another outstanding game—putting pressure on the quarterback and racking up a number of tackles. The fans had been tremendous, supporting us all night and giving us the extra help we needed. It all felt so good, and we all felt that we could really get used to this type of support.

I couldn't wait to see what the newspapers would say about the game, and I wasn't disappointed. The headline of the *Louisville Courier-Journal* article the next day (October 21, 1966) read, "Northington Leads UK Frosh Victory." It was a great story that highlighted the fact that my 103 rushing yards were the catalyst that led Kentucky to a 20–14 victory over the University of Cincinnati. It was a great way to make my first appearance in front of the fans in Lexington. I could not have written the script any better, expect maybe if I had scored on that opening kickoff return.

It was a great team effort as we pulled out the game in the last few minutes, with everyone doing an outstanding job. The UK fans were excited about our freshman team, and they felt we would have a much-improved team in 1967, when we became eligible to play varsity ball.

After the game, Coach Gray teased me, just as he would have in high school, about not going all the way on the kickoff return. He joked that I had let the yard-line stripe reach up and tackle me. He and I knew I never should have let that happen. He was just telling me to do better and get that touchdown the next time. He congratulated me for having a great game and told me how proud he was. I could tell he was pleased. My dad, who did not often verbally express his feelings, let me know he was proud as well. I could see it in his eyes and all over his face.

Some of my friends who couldn't make it to the game saw the Louisville newspaper article, and when I came home for a visit, everyone was excited and jubilant. They gave me all kinds of accolades. I was pleased that my friends had been paying attention and following my college career.

Although I did not score a touchdown, the yardage I gained running the ball had contributed to our victory. Our defense had also been stellar, with Greg having another outstanding game. My friends at Newburg and TJ never ceased to show me their love and support.

It seemed I was really on my way to success, and everything was going in the right direction, but Lady Luck has her way of turning on you at the wrong time.

The next week was another home game at Stoll Field in Lexington, and our opponent was the Vanderbilt University Commodores. Like UT, it was a member of the SEC and was in nearby Tennessee, so we were especially motivated to win that game. We had another good week of preparation, and by game time, everyone was feeling good and flying high. Because of our 2–1 record and our solid performance against Cincinnati the previous week, we had a much higher fan turnout for this game. For a freshman game, it seemed as if the stadium was full. It was the biggest crowd I had ever played in front of, and I'm sure my teammates could probably say the same.

The starting time for this game was 8:00 p.m., which gave all our students and fans, including my family and friends from Louisville, time to get there. We received an exuberant welcome as we came out from under the stadium and ran onto the field to begin the game. It was a beautiful fall evening, a great night for football. But little did I know the long-term effect this game would have on my career at UK.

I was the starting tailback on offense and a kickoff returner just as I had been in the previous game. At the beginning of the game, we moved the ball down the field very effectively, both throwing and running. I started out making several big runs right off the bat. As we marched down the field, I had several runs in which I gained anywhere from eight to twelve yards every time I touched the football. The team was blocking well, and I was really running well and thinking I would have a big game. I could sense it would only be a matter of time before I broke off a big gainer as we methodically attacked the defense.

We got down inside the fifteen-yard line, and the quarterback called my number again, a play for me to run the ball off right tackle. I was excited because it had been too long a drought since I had scored a touchdown, so I was ready to take the ball in for a score. It is good to gain a lot of yardage, but every player knows the ultimate thrill is crossing that goal line. That is what you work for, and that's how you win games and reap the rewards of all your hard work.

We ran up to the line of scrimmage, and as the quarterback barked out the snap count, I visualized the play in my mind, just as I always did. Suddenly, the center snapped the ball. I broke out of my stance and searched for a hole off the tackle spot, but no hole was in sight, so I had a decision to make. When you have the ball and eleven vicious defenders are coming to tear your head off, you have to decide quickly. With the home crowd watching, I knew I had to make this play work, but the boys from Vanderbilt had a different idea.

It became very clear that they had not come to our city just to give this game away. The closer we got to the goal, the tougher they got. In football, not only does the quarterback or anybody else with the ball have to be smart, agile, and quick but they had better be able to think and move quickly at the right times. At that moment, the plan that I had gone over in my head wasn't working because the Vanderbilt players had diagnosed the play and were plugging the hole. Once I saw that, I accelerated and broke to the outside, looking for another opening to cut up into. I needed to get to that goal line, and I was determined to score the first touchdown. Vanderbilt's linebackers and defensive backs were relentlessly pursuing me and were just as determined to keep me out of the end zone. As I sprinted toward the sideline, I realized that they had the angle on me and that my chances of beating them to the goal line and making it into the end zone were very slim.

I had two choices: I could run out of bounds or lower my shoulder, cut up, and try to get as many yards as I could. This was something I had done on numerous occasions throughout my days in football. I quickly made up my mind to cut to the goal and try to gain as many yards as I could, instead of taking the easy way out. I planted my right foot, dropped my left shoulder, exploded toward the goal line—toward the pursuers—and braced myself for impact. I met two or three tacklers in a tremendous collision.

One of the defenders hit me squarely on the shoulder, and as I went down short of the goal line, I felt a sharp pain. As I struggled to get up, the pain was so intense I could not move my left arm at all. I held that arm with my other hand as I slowly ambled off the field and to the sidelines. I headed toward our bench, and Ralph Berlin, the UK athletic trainer, met me. Seeing the expression on my face and the way I was struggling to walk, he held my arm and told me to kneel. Putting his hand under my shoulder pad, he felt my shoulder and knew immediately that it had been dislocated. He had seen this happen many times in his career.

Believe me, that shoulder injury was the absolute worst physical pain I have ever experienced. It was excruciating. Even after all these years, it seems as if it were yesterday. Every step I took as I walked to the locker room was painful. It hurt to walk, it hurt to move, and it hurt to turn. I didn't even want to talk. They had me lie on the table in the locker room as I waited for an ambulance to take me to the hospital. Once I was in the ambulance, every bump along the way caused me greater pain, and it seemed as though we would never get to the hospital. When we finally did, the doctors put me under anesthesia to put the shoulder back in place.

After I came out of recovery, somebody told me we had won the game, so I was happy about that. I did not have surgery, so I was able to go back to the football dorm the next day, with my arm in a sling.

There was no way of knowing at the time, but that shoulder injury would turn out to be one of the worst things that could have happened to me during my football career. Other than a broken nose and a broken hand in high school, I had never sustained an injury of that magnitude, so I had no idea it would plague me both physically and mentally down the road. My friend Greg was always teasing me about something, and my injury was no exception. He said, "You just went and got yourself hurt just so you could get out of practice." He was joking, of course; he knew better than that. The freshman football season was over, and we had finished with a 3–1 win-loss record, having lost only to Tennessee by one touchdown, and that with some controversy (a touchdown being called back). It had been a very successful campaign, and it gave everyone hope for an exciting and competitive varsity team in 1967.

All reports from the coaches and the news media indicated that both Greg and I had given outstanding performances as freshmen. Greg had averaged 12.5 tackles a game, which was remarkable considering that averaging 8 tackles was considered good. I had led the team in kickoff returns, with 6 for 111 yards, an average of 18.5 yards a return. I had also been the second-leading rusher, carrying the ball 33 times for 197 total yards, an average of 6 yards a carry. My longest gain had been the 41-yard touchdown against Virginia Tech. Coach Bradshaw indicated in the newspaper that both Greg and I were outstanding prospects for the varsity team the following year.

Although the Vanderbilt game had been the last for our freshman team, the varsity still had several games to go before the end of their season. The freshman players continued to practice with the varsity for the remainder of the season, but I could not participate in practice because of the shoulder. After about four weeks with my arm in a sling, I was relatively pain-free. It was back to work as usual. I began rehabbing the shoulder with light weightlifting and various range-of-motion exercises at our training facilities. I continued strengthening it as we worked out in our winter conditioning program in preparation for spring practice. Even with an injury like mine, I had no real time off from practice and conditioning sessions. If you want to play football at the highest level, you simply have to get your body and mind prepared.

After winter conditioning, we were ready to begin spring practice—one of the major differences between high school and college football. In high school I had never practiced football in the spring because unlike the Louisville city schools, the county schools where I played ball did not permit spring practice. In college, spring practice gives the players the opportunity to develop their skills and gives the coaches the opportunity to work out their plans and prepare for the fall season.

Sometime between the winter conditioning program and the beginning of spring practice, the coaches called me in to inform me that they were switching me from my tailback position on offense to defensive cornerback. I was naturally disappointed, but I tried not to show it on my face or in my body language. I wondered why they were doing this. I knew I had had an excellent first year, and I thought my performance had been as good as or better than the other running backs. I had proved my abilities, so why were they doing this? I just did not understand. Although I was not as big as some of the other backs, the weight and nutrition program and my natural maturation process had caused my weight to increase, and it was now up to about 180 pounds. Besides, I was faster and more elusive than any of the other backs.

Some of my disappointment went away after they explained their reasons for making the change. The coaches said I would be too much of a target for cheap shots by the opposition as an offensive tailback. In that position, I would be handling the ball often, thus opening myself up to being hit a lot. The coaches did not want to subject me to any unnecessary abuse from opposing teams. It was tough enough for the white players, but I would definitely be more of a target. I realized they were looking out for my well-being. As disappointed as I was, I appreciated their concern.

They didn't mention the injury to my shoulder, but I think that was a big factor in their decision. I wondered if they had seen something on the film from our Vanderbilt game, when I was injured. Had someone hit me with an illegal shot with his helmet? I never got an opportunity to see the game film, and it was probably just as well. Nothing could have been done at that point. They said I would still have an opportunity to run the ball on kickoff and punt returns, so that made me feel better, knowing I would have a chance to score some touchdowns and could still help the team—and that is the main objective, to do what you can for the team.

Spring practice began, and it wasn't long before I moved into the number-one cornerback slot because of my performance in practice and during scrimmages. Playing defense was nothing new for me, since I had played both offense and defense in high school, and I was comfortable in either position. In fact, concentrating on learning one position helped improve my skills and gave me more confidence in carrying out my assignments. As spring practice progressed, each performance became more and more impressive.

I had such an outstanding spring practice that the 1967 UK media guide put it like this: "Described as so fast and agile that he covers five yards in two strides, Nat had a tremendous spring practice. . . . In consecutive scrimmages, he returned kickoffs seventy and eighty-six yards and ran back an interception eighty-five yards—all touchdowns." That's a fair description of my spring football performance, but they forgot to mention a couple of punt returns for touchdowns. I don't want to brag, so I will forgive them for that little oversight. Seriously, I was very happy with my overall performance during spring practice, and I am certain the coaches felt the same way. Greg and I were only two of the freshmen who performed well during spring drills, and the coaches were excited about the newcomers and about the entire team's prospects for the coming season. They knew we might not be contenders for the SEC title but thought we should be very competitive and have a winning season if everyone performed up to their potential and there were no surprises.

No lingering effects from the shoulder injury the previous fall showed up in spring practice. The weightlifting and therapy during the winter had sufficiently strengthened it. Besides doing a good job returning kicks, I easily covered receivers coming into my zone by supporting our defense against running plays and tackling ball carriers coming into my territory. I would have to say I was happy with my performance, and the coaches were as well.

I often won praise from my defensive-position coach, Leon Fuller, and he indicated to my teammates that I was an example to emulate. He would point to me and say, "That is how you run, low with your body leaning forward."

He may not have known it, but that was my natural running style. Running track also helped me perfect my technique. In track, you always stayed as low as you could after exploding out of the starting blocks, building up your speed before finally rising to your normal running height. Coming up too fast slows you down and actually causes you to lose speed. In high school, I had been one of the top hurdlers in Louisville, winning my district for several years.

As spring practice ended for my freshman year, my shoulder felt good. I was reasonably sure it had healed, especially since I had not reinjured it in spring practice while taking part in all full-contact practices and scrimmages. I was ready for summer break so I could work to earn some money for clothing and other items, but things did not work out that way.

Although everything was going well on the football field, my classroom work was not up to my normal standards, and I had a couple of incompletes. I have no excuses for allowing my grades to suffer, but I guess I might have been enjoying my freshman year too much. I was enrolled in the arts and sciences curriculum and was taking routine freshman classes, but I had not declared a major. To maintain my eligibility to play as a sophomore, I had to attend summer school and take a couple of courses in recreational leadership and athletic training to bring up my grade point average. Greg also attended summer school, so we were roommates for that session as well.

We both got the grades we needed in summer school to maintain our eligibility for the fall season. I don't remember what the standards were at that time, but we were not too worried, especially since we had been excellent students. We also learned a valuable lesson about how important it was to perform well scholastically as well as athletically. We understood that no matter how great an achievement it was to be a pioneer, we needed to prepare for our futures. After summer school, we were ready to go home for a few weeks before we returned for fall football practice.

One of the distractions I faced during my freshman year was having my own car. It's not something that's advisable for a freshman in college. In fact, I almost had a tragic accident going back to school after attending one of my former high school's football games one Friday night.

I stayed longer than I should have, and as I drove down I-64 back to Lexington, I was having difficulty staying awake. I opened my windows to get air in the car, and I turned up my radio to keep me awake, but that didn't work. As I got close to Frankfort, Kentucky, I woke up to find myself only a few yards from rear-ending a semitrailer. I immediately turned my steering wheel to avoid running into the truck, and the car spun out of control. I don't remember shouting, "Jesus!" However, I am sure I did because he was the only one who could have helped me at that moment. I missed the truck, but the car was spinning in the middle of the highway, exposing me to danger from any car approaching me. The next thing I remember is the car running off the road and into the ditch, stopping with the front of the vehicle facing the wrong direction.

I was so happy to be alive that I just thanked the Lord for saving me. You may not believe in guardian angels, but I do, and mine protected me from hurt, harm, and danger that night. Although I did not realize it at the time, the Lord still had work for me to do, and this would not be the only time he protected me.

But that's not the end of this story. He still had another miracle in store for me. As I got out of the car, a middle-aged white man pulled up and also got out. He asked if I was okay, and I said yes. He said that he had seen what had happened and that he had turned around to check on me. He asked if he could help me by getting a wrecker or something, but I realized I was only several miles from Frankfort, where my cousin, Alan Haymon, was attending Kentucky State University. The gentleman gave me a ride to my cousin's dorm, and I was able to stay all night in his room. The next morning, we got a wrecker to pull my car out of the ditch, and I returned to Lexington. I had missed curfew, but I was alive and well. I still believe in miracles. I thank God for my guardian angel on the highway.

After I got home from summer school in late July or early August, I went swimming with a couple of friends. I had not been swimming in a while, and it was the first time since I had dislocated my shoulder the previous fall. I am by no means an outstanding swimmer, but I enjoy swimming and hanging out with my friends, so this was one of our favorite pastimes in the hot summer months.

On this particular day, I dived into the water and started swimming to the other side, but I turned back when I realized that I was getting tired and that I was not quite halfway across. Before I could make it back, I felt a sharp pain in my shoulder—the previously dislocated shoulder. The more I swam, the more pain I felt, and I realized my only way to get back was to use every swimming technique I knew and to pray a lot. I finally made it safely out of the water, but the damage to my shoulder had been done. I was thankful that God had been right there to help me survive that scare. I would not have made it without his divine protection.

After I got out of the water, I still felt a sharp pain in my shoulder. I could not tell how much damage I had done, but I was very concerned. By the time I got home though, the shoulder was feeling better, so I did not have it checked out by a doctor. That was the end of my swimming for the summer, and my only hope was that the shoulder would be okay. Only time and rest would determine that. Mainly I was just thankful that my guardian angel had been looking out for me that day.

After these two frightening incidents my freshman year, you would think that nothing else could possibly happen that would cause me so much emotional grief. The rest of my summer break was fast coming to an end, and soon it would be time to pack my things and head back down I-64 to Lexington, UK, and fall football practice. It was time for Greg and me to begin our sophomore year and become members of the varsity team. We would make history by becoming the first African Americans to play in the SEC. Of course, we had no idea how that would affect us, but we were both prepared for and excited about the opportunity to play the game we loved so much. Breaking the color barrier that had existed for so long would be a remarkable achievement. And it would be a tremendous blessing for both Blacks and whites. We couldn't wait to get back to campus and continue the journey we had started the previous year. I could not imagine what that would be like, but I was ready to give it my best shot, and I had no doubt that we would be successful.

8

The Walkout

As summer school roommates, Greg Page and I spent endless hours sharing our feelings about our first year at Kentucky. It turned out that we were both a little discouraged and disenchanted for several reasons. First, because we had to attend summer school and forgo making some much-needed money working full-time jobs. Second, because the UK sports program did not seem to be recruiting other African American football players aggressively enough. Many of the conversations between Greg and me revolved around our status as the first two Black football players in the SEC and our feelings about the coaches' failure to recruit more Black athletes.

When they recruited Greg and me, the coaches had assured us they would be going after other Black players, but it was not happening fast enough for us. The promise to recruit other African Americans was one of the major reasons we had accepted the opportunity to play at UK and in the SEC. During the summer of 1967, Greg and I had helped UK recruit and sign two other African American players, Wilbur Hackett, an All-State and All-American fullback/linebacker from Louisville duPont Manual High School, and Houston Hogg, an All-American fullback from Owensboro, Kentucky. Another Black player, Albert Johnson, one of my former team-mates from TJ, joined the team as a walk-on. We were happy to have these three aboard to help us, but when we saw all the talented Black high school players who had come to Lexington to participate in the East-West All-Star game the summer after our freshman year and realized that the majority had not been recruited by UK, we became discouraged. I guess we didn't think that maybe those players were more interested in playing for the Big Ten or other major conferences than in dealing with the additional pressure of integrating the SEC.

To say Hackett and Hogg were outstanding would be an understatement. They had proved themselves. Signing two or three Blacks at a time, however, was not the kind of recruiting we expected, and it certainly wasn't enough to give Kentucky the kind of athletic ammunition it desperately needed to compete favorably.

We believed that the coaches were not living up to their commitment and that we needed to get their attention. Greg and I thought we should do something to express our disappointment. One day while we were still in summer school, we decided to leave campus, thinking maybe we would quit or transfer to some other university. Since the All-Star guys seemed happy and excited to be going to other conferences, maybe we needed to follow them. We did not have much of a plan; we were just frustrated, and we wanted more help. We packed our belongings and left Lexington, traveling together to Louisville. We explained our feelings to my parents and said that we were thinking about leaving UK. They told us that they understood our frustration but that we really needed to think about it and not make any rash decisions. After a day or two, Greg left Louisville and went home to Middlesboro.

We were not home long before the coaches called and wanted to talk. We set up a meeting so we could express our feelings and they could do the same. When we met with the coaches, Greg told them, "If we're going to do this [integrate the SEC], we'll need help." They understood our position, and they assured us they were doing all they could to recruit the best players, including African Americans, for the team. Greg and I felt better about their commitment during the meeting, and we decided to return to school and be a little more patient.

In addition to assisting in the recruitment of Wilbur Hackett and Houston Hogg, we also helped recruit Jim Green, a high school All-American track star from Eminence, Kentucky, for the UK track team. Green became a world-class sprinter and was one of the first African American track stars in the SEC. He is now in the UK Hall of Fame. Hackett, the first African American to be named captain of the football team (1970), was inducted into the UK Football Hall of Fame and was recognized in 2013 as an SEC Legend. He also worked as an SEC football official for many years.

That fall, even though we felt that things could have been better both on and off the field, Greg and I were committed to helping our school become a contender in the SEC in any way we could. After our brief boycott, we felt good about our relationship with the coaches and our teammates. We had seen progress and believed that everyone was committed to the cause we were playing for. But things would change and become so discouraging once Greg and I were no longer there that Wilbur Hackett and Houston Hogg said the officials were doing nothing to recruit Black players. And in 1968, no Black football players were signed by Kentucky. Hackett and Hogg would later begin assisting the coaches in the recruitment of African American athletes, especially after a new head football coach, John Ray, was hired in 1969.

When summer break was over, I packed up my car and headed back to Lexington for football camp and my sophomore year in school. That year, we would not be staying in Wildcat Manor. Not only that, but the freshmen, including Wilbur Hackett, Houston Hogg, and Albert Johnson, would no longer reside in Kitten Lodge. It was probably because of the NCAA rule changes designed to limit preferential treatment for athletes. As a result, we had to stay in the regular student dorm. Unlike in Kitten Lodge, there would be only two people assigned to a room. Of course, Greg and I would share a room again.

Coming into the camp was exciting because now we were eligible to play varsity. This meant we would officially break the color barrier in the game against Mississippi on September 30, 1967. However, that was far from our minds as we checked out our new dorm room. It would be different mingling with the other students more and eating in the student cafeteria. After the long summer, it was good to see the teammates we had played with as freshmen: Phil Thompson, Marty New, Cary Shahid, and the others. Although our team would be young, with the success we had as freshmen, everyone had high expectations for the team in 1967.

In a September 3, 2004, *Los Angeles Times* newspaper article, Wilbur Hackett stated that as soon as he arrived at training camp as a freshman, he understood why Page and I had asked for help. He talked about how the football team members were kept apart from the other students. Although he felt that things were good for the most part, he had noticed a lack of acceptance among some players, mainly because they had never gone to school or interacted with Blacks. Hackett said Page and I had found other ways to cope. "They were super tight," he said. "They helped each other and they were always talking to us."

When we began fall football practice, the priority for the first few days' workouts was getting into top condition, and there was little full contact. Greg and I started just as we had left off in the spring, doing an excellent job and living up to everyone's expectations. Although we were not yet tackling, my shoulder seemed to be fully recovered, and everything was going according to expectations for both of us. We were definitely going to be instrumental in helping the team become a winner.

Then things began to fall apart.

The first sign of that deterioration was the reoccurrence of my shoulder problem. Right after we began some minor contact, my shoulder popped out of place when I tackled a ball carrier. Physically, it was not as painful as the original injury, but mentally, it was more painful, especially since I had gone through the entire spring drills without having any problems whatsoever. Now, to have the shoulder pop out of place again was very upsetting. The coaches and trainer thought a little therapy and a few days with no contact would allow it to heal and everything would be fine. I don't know if anyone actually realized the full extent of my original injury, but now I had to deal with the impairment all over again.

That reinjured shoulder became a huge problem. The coaches decided to move me again to another position, from cornerback to safety, so I could restrict the use of that arm. With that change, I was able to continue practicing the next day, and I could do everything in practice except take part in full contact.

"Thomas Jefferson football star Nate Northington signed with the University of Kentucky yesterday and became the first Negro athlete ever to sign a Southeastern Conference athletic grant-in-aid." (The *Courier-Journal* archives, December 20, 1965.)

I am in the front; behind me, from left to right, are Governor Breathitt; Charlie Bradshaw, UK coach; Jim Gray, high school coach; Dr. John W. Oswald, president of UK. (University of Kentucky archives, December 1965.)

Dad and Mom's fiftieth wedding anniversary. (Author's personal collection.)

This mile marker stands at the corner of Virginia Avenue and I-264. (Author's personal collection.)

The picture shows me, Muhammad Ali, and Will Seay at the Louisville Metro Housing Authority in 2002. (Author's personal collection.)

NBA Hall of Famer and University of Louisville All-American Wes Unseld, Tony Seay, and me. Picture taken around January 1968 in front of the Seay house. (Author's personal collection.)

By my sophomore year at Thomas Jefferson High School, I was known as a star on the football team. This photo was taken right before practice. (The *Courier-Journal* archives, 1963.)

I am second from left as I, Jim Callahan, and Ron Gathright receive final instructions from Coach Jim Gray. (The *Courier-Journal* archives, 1963.)

1964 Thomas Jefferson baseball team. I am fourth from the left in the front row, between Bob Redman and Jim Dewalt. (Author's personal collection.)

I aim for two points while Bob Redmon, Ron Gathright, and Jim Dewalt get into position for a rebound. (Author's personal collection, 1966.)

My Thomas Jefferson High School senior photo. (Author's personal collection, 1966.)

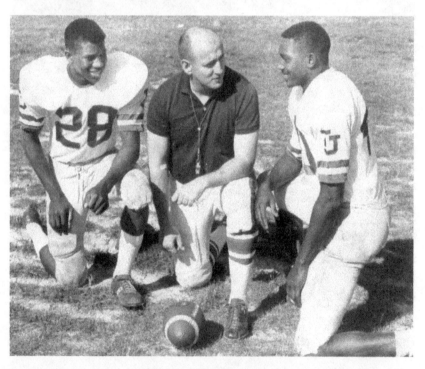

"Coach Jim Gray of Thomas Jefferson has Jefferson County's No. 1 and No. 2 scorers in halfback Nate Northington and fullback Ron Gathright." (The *Courier-Journal* archives, October 20, 1965.)

"Jim Hudson (left) reserve fullback taking some teasing from TJ stars Nate Northington (standing) and Ron Gathright." (The *Courier-Journal* archives, September 27, 1965.)

"West Backfield Starters. Starting for the West in Saturday night's (Saturday, August 6, 1966) high-school All-Star game will be, from left, halfback Nat Northington of Thomas Jefferson, halfback Ira Glass of St. Xavier, quarterback Oscar Brohm of Flaget, and fullback Ron Gathright of Thomas Jefferson." (*Lexington Herald-Leader* archives.)

West Defenders. The West All-Stars defensive unit: (front row, left to right) end Clint Walker of Trinity, tackle Greg Karem of Seneca, linebacker Ben Baker of Male, linebacker David Bratcher of Flaget; (second row) linebacker Mike Houston of Franklin-Simpson, me as a corner linebacker of Thomas Jefferson, end Lee Bouggess of Shawnee, tackle Phillip Hubbert of Madisonville; (back row) halfback Franklin Foreman of Manual, safety Steve Doran of Murray, halfback Ira Glass of St. Xavier. *Herald-Leader* staff photo published August 6, 1966. (*Lexington Herald-Leader* archives.)

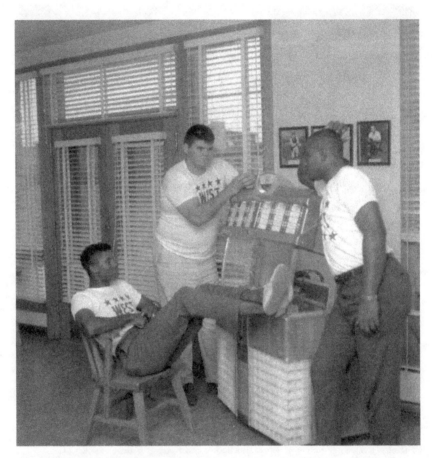

"Nat Northington, left, the first Negro to sign a University of Kentucky football grant, props himself on a juke box at Wildcat Manor August 2, 1966, with West All-Star teammates Mike McClure of Mayfield and Melvin Cross of Louisville Central." (*Lexington Herald-Leader* archives.)

West High School All-Star game team (August 6, 1966) in Lexington, Kentucky. I am number 34, second row. Ron Gathright is number 41, second row. (Author's personal collection.)

UK assistant coach George Boone; Mom, Flossie Northington; Edward T. Breathitt, governor of Kentucky; and my high school coach, Jim Gray, saw me make history by signing UK and SEC athletic scholarship on October 19, 1965. The governor's signature on the picture reads "To Nat Northington, Outstanding student and athlete with best wishes, Edward T. Breathitt, Governor of Kentucky." (Author's personal collection.)

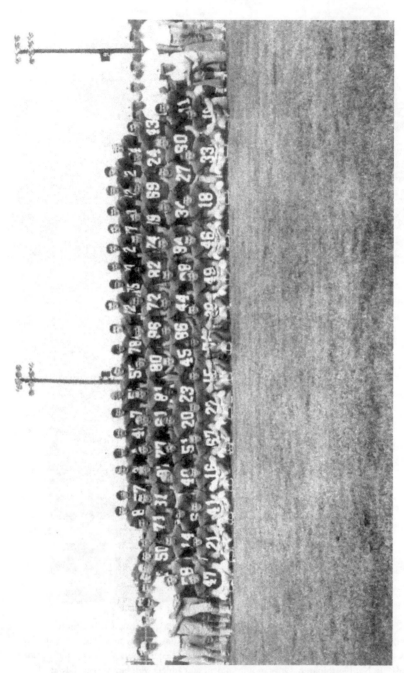

University of Kentucky varsity football team, 1967; I am number 23 and Greg Page is number 82. (University of Kentucky archives.)

Photo of Kentucky's old Stoll Field/McLean Stadium in 1967, where I broke the color barrier against Ole Miss. Next door is Memorial Coliseum, the basketball arena. (Author's personal collection.)

My high school "who's who" yearbook picture, 1966. (Author's personal collection.)

"UK's Nat Northington during practice at Lexington." (The *Courier-Journal* archives, April 11, 1967.)

"UK Athletes Gain Know-How. Turning to Umpiring? . . . Greg Page of Middlesboro (right) and Louisville Nat Northington (center), who this fall will be the first Negro varsity football players at the University of Kentucky, are taking a course in recreation leadership. Here Page gives the out sign as Erick Johnson tags Gay Martin during a Little Mite practice at Lexington's Douglass Park. Watching is Sam Adams of the city recreation department." (*Lexington Herald-Leader* archives, July 16, 1967.)

Kentucky's Greg Page during practice in Lexington. (University of Kentucky archives, 1967.)

Greg Page in official UK team blazer and tie. (University of Kentucky archives, 1967.)

"UK's Nat Northington during practice at Lexington." (University of Kentucky archives, 1967.)

Here I am, number 42, outrunning the last man for a game-winning seventy-seven-yard touchdown. We outscored Eastern Kentucky University in a 19–7 homecoming victory, October 27, 1970. (Author's personal collection.)

WESTERN KENTUCKY UNIVERSITY

1970 - OHIO VALLEY CONFERENCE CHAMPIONS
WON - 8   LOST - 1   TIED - 1

Western Kentucky	30	Indiana State	6	Western Kentucky	19	*Eastern Kentucky	7
Western Kentucky	28	*Austin Peay	9	Western Kentucky	24	*Morehead State	14
Western Kentucky	10	*East Tennessee	10	Western Kentucky	13	*Middle Tennessee	17
Western Kentucky	45	Eastern Michigan	6	Western Kentucky	14	Butler	0
Western Kentucky	28	*Tennessee Tech	0	Western Kentucky	33	*Murray State	7

*Ohio Valley Conference game

Western Kentucky University's Ohio Valley Conference Championship football team. I am in the front row, second from left. Romeo Crennel, former coach of the Cleveland Browns and Kansas City Chiefs, and holder of five Super Bowl rings, is in the last row, fourth from the right. (Author's personal collection.)

"We Are Family." Bottom (left to right): my sister Barbara Montgomery, Mom, Dad, my sister Rose Packer, my nephew Courtney Montgomery; top (left to right): brothers James, William Jr., me, Kenneth, and Michael, 1978. (Author's personal collection.)

With wife Gwen at daughter Teresa's wedding, May 2007. (Author's personal collection.)

With wife Gwen at a restaurant in 2007. (Author's personal collection.)

With wife Gwen, attending daughter Kecia's college graduation. (Author's personal collection.)

Praising the Lord at Newburg Apostolic Church with some of the brothers in the background. (Author's personal collection.)

Photo of the inaugural recipients of the SEC Commissioner Michael L. Slive Distinguished Service Award, with Wilbur Hackett Jr.; me; Godfrey Dillard; Commissioner Michael L. Slive; cousin of Perry Wallace; Melvin Page, brother of Greg Page; and Houston Hogg. Dillard and Wallace of Vanderbilt University were the first Black basketball players in the SEC. Page, Hackett, Hogg, and I were the first Black football players in the SEC. Houston Hogg passed away in 2020, Michael L. Slive in 2018, Perry Wallace in 2017, and Greg Page in 1967. (Courtesy of SEC Commissioner Office.)

Black SEC Legends who integrated SEC football and basketball pose on the field during the SEC Championship football game. Cousin representing Perry Wallace, basketball, Vanderbilt; Mel Page, brother of Greg Page; Wilbur Hackett Jr., football, Kentucky; Bo Jackson, Heisman trophy winner, football, Auburn; me; Herschel Walker, Heisman trophy winner, football, Georgia; and Godfrey Dillard, basketball, Vanderbilt. (Courtesy of SEC Commissioner Office.)

Here I am receiving my SEC Legends and Distinguished Service Awards from SEC Commissioner Greg Sankey. It was a tremendous honor to receive this recognition as a trailblazer for SEC sports. I did not see this coming fifty years after my integrating the SEC. (Courtesy of SEC Commissioner Office.)

A screenshot of me giving the acceptance speech for all fourteen recipients of the SEC Legends Class of 2017. The MC felt I should be the one giving the speech since I was the only one of the recipients to receive a standing ovation after my introduction as the first Black football player in the SEC. The ovation was moving, giving me chills and gratification to be honored and appreciated for my accomplishments. (Courtesy of SEC Commissioner Office.)

Here I am with University of Kentucky athletics director Mitch Barnhart, holding the trophy recognizing me as an SEC Legend. I was appreciative to Mitch and the university for submitting my name to the SEC for this recognition. To be included with the hundreds of tremendous athletes and the administration that have made the SEC the most successful athletic conference in America is a tremendous honor. When I think of the many All-Conference, All-American, and Heisman Trophy winners that have played in the conference, I am overwhelmed. But none of those can claim the distinction as the first Black player. I give God all the glory. (Author's personal collection.)

Receiving greetings from head University of Kentucky football coach Mark Stoops doing the Catwalk preceding the game at Kroger Field commemorating the fiftieth anniversary of integrating the University of Kentucky and Southeastern Conference football. I don't know where the time has gone. It does not seem as though fifty years has passed since that historical day on September 30, 1967. (Author's personal collection.)

It was a tremendous honor to walk onto Kroger Field for the pregame coin toss as the honorary captain before the fiftieth anniversary game on September 30, 2017. It was fifty years ago when I ran onto the old Stoll Field at UK and broke the color barrier at the University of Kentucky and SEC in the game against Ole Miss. Unfortunately, Greg Page, my copioneer and trailblazer, passed away the previous evening on September 29, 1967. Greg, this honor was for you as well. (Courtesy of University of Kentucky Athletics.)

With the University of Kentucky Athletic Hall of Fame inductees. The 2015 class included Andy Green, baseball; Lisa Breiding Duerr, cross-country/track; Jared Lorenzen, football; Taryn Ignacio Patrick, women's swimming/diving; Antoine Walker, men's basketball; Greg Page, football, posthumously; and me, football. It was an unbelievable experience and honor to receive a phone call from Athletics Director Mitch Barnhart notifying me of my selection. During his closing remarks, Mitch announced that the Athletics Department would dedicate a statue in 2016 to honor the Black trailblazers who integrated UK and SEC football. Jared Lorenzen passed away in 2019, and Greg Page in 1967. (Courtesy of University of Kentucky Athletics.)

Giving my UK Hall of Fame induction speech. I am so thankful and grateful I was one of the people chosen by Almighty God to help bring people of different races, ethnicities, and colors together through the game of football. Sports has been one of the avenues used by God to bring people together. Our lives are much more fulfilling and enjoyable as a result of breaking the color barrier in our country. I owe Him all the glory. Excerpts from my acceptance speech are included in the introduction. (Author's personal collection.)

Here we are at the statue dedication ceremony. This is the culmination of a day full of tremendous honor and recognition. The entire University of Kentucky administration is to be commended and applauded for this awesome and astounding recognition. This is truly an unbelievable and remarkable act of gratitude. We felt loved and appreciated beyond words at this act of love by all those who made this possible. We truly could not express our gratitude and our feelings sufficiently. All we could say was thank you to everyone who made this recognition a reality. Pictured in the photo are Mel Page, me, Wilbur Hackett Jr., and Houston Hogg. You can read my speech in the introduction. Houston Hogg passed away in 2020 and Greg Page in 1967. (Courtesy of University of Kentucky Athletics.)

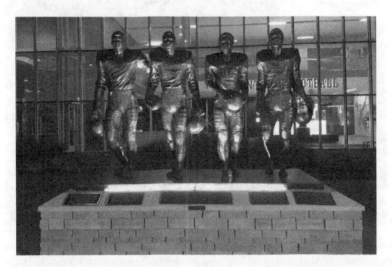

Night view of the historical statue in front of the UK training facility recognizing the four University of Kentucky and SEC trailblazers. Included in the statue are Greg Page, me, Wilbur Hackett Jr., and Houston Hogg. (Courtesy of University of Kentucky Athletics.)

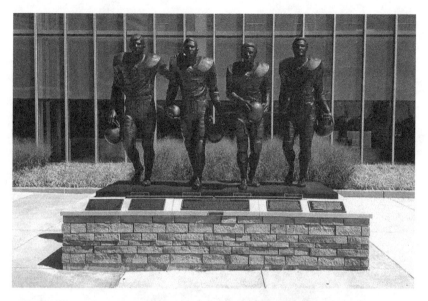

Daytime view of the historical statue recognizing the four University of Kentucky and SEC football trailblazers. (Courtesy of University of Kentucky Athletics.)

Attending a basketball game with Gwen at Rupp Arena as a guest of the university. I was being recognized as an SEC Legend during halftime, along with other honorees. It was very exhilarating to be recognized and given a roaring ovation from the usual sellout. We were treated to a great match as the Cats won an exciting, closely fought game. It had been some time since I attended a basketball game at the university. Gwen saw her first game and was overwhelmed by the festivities. (Author's personal collection.)

Attending the annual Wildcats Athletics CATSBY Recognition Awards with Mitch Barnhart and Wilbur Hackett. We were excited to receive a beautiful oil painting and metal replica of the trailblazer statue. This was my first CATSBY event where all athletics were recognized. I also had the opportunity to meet and have a photo taken with UK head basketball coach John Calipari. (Author's personal collection.)

Wearing number 23 as a UK sophomore. I wore number 21 as a freshman, but my number
was changed to 23 my sophomore year. I was unaware it would be changed, but I did not
make a fuss about it, as I never felt the number on my uniform would affect my game;
however, I can say I wore number 23 before it became a chosen number by some of the
greatest athletes (i.e., Michael Jordan, Kobe Bryant, Anthony Davis). Athletes today seem
more concerned about their number than during my playing days, or maybe it was just me.
Some even pay to have their preferred number. (Courtesy of University of Kentucky Libraries
Special Collections Research Center.)

Attending the Kentucky Sports Hall of Fame ceremony. (Author's personal collection.)

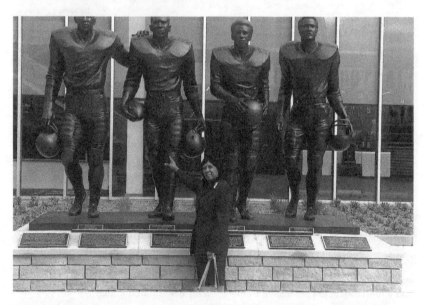

Gwen pointing to my image on the trailblazer statue. She was very proud of my accomplishment and was my greatest supporter and publicist. She would always be the first to point out my achievements to unknowing and inquisitive persons, often saying, "Do you know who he is and what he did?" Then she would proudly share with those who would graciously listen. I was so appreciative of her never-ending adoration and love. I thank God for blessing me with such a wonderful helpmate. I was truly blessed to have her in my life. (Author's personal collection.)

Wearing number 21 as a freshman. My number was changed to 23 as a sophomore. Maybe I should share some credit for making 23 such a sought-after number in sports over the past three decades. UK basketball great Anthony Davis helped make it famous as well. (Courtesy of University of Kentucky Libraries Special Collections Research Center.)

Attending the viewing of the *Black in Blue* documentary at the UK Student Center with members of the Greg Page family. The film was produced by University of Kentucky alumni Paul Wagner and Paul Karem. Karem is also a former UK football player. The film chronicles the story of the integration of UK and SEC football by the four Black trailblazers. The film has been shown on the Kentucky Education Television (KET) network. This is the second documentary film on this subject; the first was *Forward Progress: The Integration of SEC Football*, produced by Blake Berson and Jack Ford, and shown on CBS Sports Network. (Author's personal collection.)

On vacation with Gwen. It was always a joy to get away and spend time alone after such a demanding schedule at work. I realize now more than ever how important that time was for our relationship and for our memories. I am truly grateful that God gave us those precious times and memories. (Author's personal collection.)

Family gathering for Thanksgiving dinner. This is a blessed occasion when we get together to give thanks for the family we have been blessed with, and for all God has provided our family with. (Author's personal collection.)

With Gwen in front of the trailblazer statue. "To God be the Glory"! (Author's personal collection.)

Holding award along with granddaughter Jayla proudly holding a UK helmet at the SEC Legends ceremony, with Gwen, Nate Jr., and Juwan, all proud of Dad. (Author's personal collection.)

Attending church service and giving God the glory! Mom and Dad, brother William Jr., sister Barbara, and host of nephews and nieces. (Author's personal collection.)

Shaking hands with my pastor, Waverly J. Holland, who has been a spiritual father and mentor in my life for many years. He has been an exemplary, true man of God and one who chose me to serve as assistant pastor under his leadership. He is a sincere servant of God and a man to whom I am very grateful. It is because of his leadership I feel I am a better Christian today. I am thankful for him taking me under his wing and showing me how a man of God carries himself. (Author's personal collection.)

Sunday church service with Gwen and daughter Renee, Sean, Thomas, and Keenan. Always grateful to be able to spend time with family worshiping and giving thanks for all our blessings. (Author's personal collection.)

MEET THE "KITTENS

NORTHINGTON   PAGE

NAT NORTHINGTON—Alternating as the Kittens' tailback, Nat has lived up to the All-State reputation gained at Thomas Jefferson High in Louisville . . . The slender Negro, first of his race to gain athletic scholarship at UK, gained over 2,000 yards and 194 points in final two years as school-boy star . . . Scored 41-yard touchdown in Kitten's rout of Virginia Tech frosh and broke away for 32-yard kickoff return versus Baby Vols.

GREG PAGE—Trained for future football greatness by Coach Walt Green at Middlesboro High, Greg performed at end in aiding the Yellow Jackets to a 10-2 record in '65 and state runner-up honors in Class AA . . . The husky Negro won All-State honors and was MVP of conference (SEKC) . . . Also played basketball, track and baseball . . . Sizes up at 6-2½, 192.

Picture and write-up included in a program from a varsity game at UK Stoll Field in 1965. Freshmen were ineligible to play on the varsity at this time but were introduced to the fans by means of the programs. The freshman team was affectionately given the name "Kittens." It was neat having your photo and write-up included in the program, giving the fans an opportunity to get to know your background and accomplishments. (Author's personal collection.)

Receiving a prayer of consecration during one of my church's council meetings.
(Author's personal collection.)

Four generations of Northingtons. God is truly faithful, and I am so thankful to have such a lovely family. (Author's personal collection.)

Here I am at my surprise seventieth birthday celebration with my grandchildren as they ham it up for the camera. Gwen did a good job of trying to surprise me, and I graciously went along with it. I was surprised that my sister Barbara traveled over a thousand miles to help me celebrate. That is real love. It was a terrific birthday party, with many friends and family. I am truly blessed. (Author's personal collection.)

With Gwen, Jayla, and sister Rose attending the fiftieth anniversary celebration game at Kroger Field. (Author's personal collection.)

Here I am giving my Kentucky Sports Hall of Fame induction speech at the Galt House in Louisville. I am honored for receiving this tremendous award. Also present was a number of staff from the University of Kentucky Athletics Department, including assistant athletics directors DeWayne Peevy and William Neely. (Courtesy of the Louisville Sports Commission.)

Photo of the 2019 Kentucky Sports Hall of Fame recipients: Ralph Hacker, UK sports
announcer; Deion Branch, University of Louisville and New England Patriots great; me; Derek
Anderson, University of Kentucky and NBA great; and Karl F. Schmitt Jr., president and CEO
of the Kentucky Sports Hall of Fame. (Courtesy of the Louisville Sports Commission.)

9

In Due Season

For many years, the Greg Page accident was something I could not talk about, and I didn't even want to think about it. The day began like any other day since the beginning of fall football camp. It was a typical hot, sunny, humid August day in Lexington, Kentucky. We got up for breakfast, still sore from the previous day's practice. We lounged around—giving the food time to digest—before finally walking to the practice facilities to dress and prepare for another tough day of football practice. We were just trying to keep our minds occupied and maintain positive attitudes. Greg was his usual jovial self, always upbeat and optimistic. If you were down for any reason, Greg had a way of lifting your spirits. As we made our way out onto the practice field, there was nothing in the world that could have prepared us for what would take place that day.

The day's practice started just like any other. It was August 22, 1967, and we were preparing for the first game against Indiana University (IU).

In a *Los Angeles Times* article from September 3, 2004, staff writer David Wharton described the event like this: "The kid from a small mining town in eastern Kentucky was so strong, bigger than life, no one could quite fathom what had happened. . . . Maybe someone tripped him from behind and he hit the ballcarrier funny. Maybe he slipped and someone fell on him." Wharton was trying to explain the chain of events that led to Greg Page's tragic injury on that day on UK's practice field, just a few days into fall football practice. Wharton interviewed Jeff Van Note, the future NFL All-Pro who had been the first team defensive end ahead of Greg Page.

As the second-string defensive end behind Van Note, Greg was expected to play in the season opener against Indiana University and to help provide depth to the defensive line throughout the entire season. However, that wouldn't happen, because everything changed that day.

The defensive squad was running a pursuit drill in shorts and shoulder pads, which called for the defenders to pursue the ball carrier, just give him a bump, and stop. Typically, the coaches used this time to get the players oriented to football again after the long summer break. They did not let the players engage in full contact until their bodies had adjusted. The eleven-man offense was not taking part in the drill, which was designed to be run at less than full speed. According to various reports, when the pileup cleared after one of these drills, Greg Page remained on the ground with a devastating injury and did not move. His neck had been broken, and he was paralyzed. Van Note indicated that he did not know what had happened, stating, "It was such a freak thing."

Unaware of Greg's injury, I was practicing with the defensive backs on another part of the field. Activity in the area where Greg was had slowed down. I assumed practice was over when the coaches called all the players into a big group and had us get down on one knee.

What made this unusual was that we had not run wind sprints as we usually did at the end of practice. We knew that either something had happened or the coaches wanted to make an important announcement. I don't even remember what I thought it might be, but never in a million years would I have expected to hear what the coach said. We were not prepared for that announcement.

Coach Bradshaw was solemn as he informed us that a tragic accident had occurred. He said Greg had been injured and taken to the hospital. We were devastated, but still, I hoped for the best. Later in the locker room, as we showered and dressed, some of the players who had seen the accident tried to explain what had happened. I was surprised to hear varying accounts. It's funny how nine or ten people can be in the same place and each see something very different, especially in an emergency.

They did agree that as he lay on the ground with the training staff attending to him, he was motionless. A few hours later, we found out that Greg was paralyzed from the neck down. This was simply unbelievable.

Like most of the others on the team, I had never experienced anything like this in my life.

I didn't know exactly what the paralysis would mean or how it would affect him. I could only pray for his recovery. I went back to the dorm that night and prayed for my friend as I had never prayed before. I realized it was all in God's hands, but I could not understand how something like this could happen. In life, we don't know what will happen, nor do we know what trials we will face, but we must trust in him in every situation. I did not quite understand any of this as a nineteen-year-old.

The next day, it seemed to be business as usual for the Wildcats. It was as though we could not afford to take a day off. We went right back onto the football field and began practicing again to prepare for the upcoming game against Indiana. My body was there, but that was about all, as my mind was in the hospital with Greg. Somehow I made it through the practice and the day, and it was back to the dorm room. That was the routine every day. There was no counseling of any kind. During that time, grief counseling was not common. I was left to endure the tragedy on my own, and my teammates and I talked about it very little. I guess they did not know how to cope with something of this magnitude, and it seemed that the coaches didn't either.

Every day the coaches would come out and update us on Greg's condition, which remained unchanged. His neck was broken, and doctors feared that operating on it would do more damage. He was in traction and on a ventilator. His condition was critical, and all we could do was pray he would make it. We prayed individually and as a team, but the reports did not give us much hope.

At first, only his parents and Coach Bradshaw were allowed to see him in the hospital—that is, until Greg insisted that the hospital allow me to visit. I was extremely glad he did, and I mustered up a little more hope. I was not sure what to expect, but I was just happy to have a chance to see my friend. When I walked into the room, I was not prepared for what I saw. He had metal rods going into his skull to keep his head immobile. He was on breathing machines and had lost considerable weight. He was so frail and had changed so much in such a short period. I had only seen people in traction on television, never in person. Although I was devastated, I knew I had to be strong for him and not show it.

I tried to speak as positively as I could. I told him the team was praying for him and encouraged him to keep the faith. I reminded him that God would take care of him. Even in that hospital bed, paralyzed with a broken neck, Greg was amazingly optimistic. In fact, his attitude encouraged me. I thought I was a person of faith, but there I was being encouraged by the person who was totally immobile and fighting with everything he had. He expressed concern for his teammates and didn't want us to worry. He wanted us to be strong, because in the end everything would be all right. He was even concerned about missing practice and classes. He was looking forward to getting out of the hospital and getting back to UK.

Greg was truly a person of great faith. His parents told him he must have faith in three things—his nurse, his doctor, and God. They spoke to him about patience and the courage he would need to make it through a long fight if necessary, and he responded well.

The players who were closest to Greg wanted to visit him as well; however, they were not able to do so. I believe it was a decision meant to help Greg maintain as positive a mental and spiritual attitude as he possibly could. I'm sure it was a joint decision by all those who cared about Greg the most. I only had the opportunity to visit him that once, and I am grateful for that chance to see him one last time.

When I went back to my room, I could not help but break down. Every day after practice, I would sit there in the empty, lonely dorm room, thinking about Greg fighting for his life in that hospital bed, and all I could do was pray for God to work a miracle. Greg and I had been nearly inseparable since we came to UK as freshmen. All our good times together would flash through my mind when I was alone. We had supported each other, and now that support was gone. I did not have anyone with whom I could share my feelings, and nobody offered any counseling or intervention to help me deal with this tragedy. Even though my teammates were there with me, it was as if I were alone on the practice field, and in a sense, except for God, I really was.

Greg's injury was not the only devastating injury that year. Amazingly, only two weeks after that day, a freshman, Cecil New, my old roommate Marty's brother, broke his neck during a scrimmage on Stoll Field and was paralyzed from the waist down. Because of my shoulder, I did not participate in the scrimmage, so I saw the accident take place on the field. Everyone associated with the team was once again devastated. What was going on? What was happening to us? It was hard when I read in the paper that Cecil had succumbed to his injury.

I am sure the news media and UK officials and fans must have thought back to the football team's one-year probation in April 1964 after the NCAA's investigation of UK's off-season program in June 1963.

In the December 15, 2007, edition of the *Cats' Pause*, Russell Rice, long-time UK employee, wrote, "The black shadow that hovered over Charlie Bradshaw's head first appeared in 1963, when *Sports Illustrated* exposed his brutal . . . training methods." Rice said that a player had sustained a head injury, remained in a coma after undergoing two surgeries, and spent three months in the hospital.

The article noted that the NCAA apparently felt that too many players were being injured in practice, and a large number of players were quitting the team. Rice said that after one loss, Bradshaw held a "brutal" scrimmage, during which a number of players were injured. This led university president John Oswald to demand an explanation, and he even had a group of doctors and the UK team physician look at the practice films. Rice said the practices continued as usual even though Oswald monitored them.

In his article, Rice quoted Phil Thompson, an All-State wide receiver from Louisville who was Greg's and my roommate when we were freshmen. Thompson said that he believed the conditions and methods in place for the team had led to twenty-one out of thirty scholarship players from the 1966 freshman team leaving the squad. The squad had four high school All-Americans.

Of course, I was unaware of the 1963 NCAA investigation and subsequent probation at the time of Greg's injury, and I can't say how I would have reacted if I had known. Nothing could have changed his condition, and all I know is that we were young men out to play college football, and we worked as hard as we were required, and I can't say whether practice at UK was tougher or more brutal than other programs. We were just doing our jobs in a game that we loved.

Most people have exaggerated the degree of racial hostility Greg and I may have experienced at UK. Although not everything was a bed of roses,

I'm sometimes shocked when I read things about us and about the events surrounding Greg's injury. Some people questioned how he could have been hurt in a simple pursuit drill that we had run many times. Other people wondered if "they" had given the ball to Greg intentionally and planned the whole thing. I don't know the answers to all those questions. All I know is that Greg never told me anybody hated him or had threatened him in any way.

A little intrateam rivalry or even some natural jealousy may have been at work because Greg excelled at the game. He easily could have outshone most of the other players, no matter what color they were. Little rivalries are common among players, and they usually mean nothing.

I know it doesn't make a good, juicy story, but I do not have any reason to believe anyone wanted Greg or me to get hurt. If there was a racial problem on the team during my college years, it was well concealed. Nobody treated us as if we were less than the white players. I don't recall anybody referring to me by any racial slurs or using them in my presence.

I have been called the N-word, but that was off the field and away from football. I recall one minor incident at UK. I don't remember who it was, but at one point someone made note of one of my white teammates, whose last name was Koon. We were all sitting around, getting ready for practice, when another player, who happened to be white, laughed and said, "Well, I see we have three 'coons' on the team," invoking a derogatory term for Blacks. For the record, he was wrong, since the team had only one Koon, and that was neither Greg nor me.

As I recall, that was his attempt at humor, but there wasn't much laughter behind it, and he seemed to regret that he had said it. As I said earlier, the coaches didn't play when it came to racism. It was not allowed, and you had better believe nobody else even tried it. The strongest thing I can say is that they were insensitive, and I don't know if it was intentional or due to a lack of experience, knowledge, and compassion. I believe it was a combination of all those factors.

As painful as Greg's injury was—and even now, it's not easy to think or talk about—I still hold no grudges, anger, or suspicion in my heart toward anyone. The majority of the players on my team treated me with respect, and, if anything, some may have protected me from problems. So, for the record, Nate Northington doesn't blame anyone and has never believed that Greg's injury was anything more than an accident, just as Cecil New's was.

I understand that because of the overall racial climate during that time, it is natural for people to raise questions, but football is a brutal sport. Players suffer injuries in almost every practice and in every game, and it is only the grace of God that protects most from tragedy.

John McGill, the *Lexington Herald* sports editor, in his column on October 4, 1967, said that Mr. and Mrs. Robert Page, Greg's parents, did not blame anyone for the accident. "We are not embittered at football," Mr. Page said. He explained that Greg had loved the game of football and that he would have been a bad parent if he had prevented him from playing the game he loved. He said the injury could have occurred anywhere Greg went to play football.

The UK coaches and officials, as well as many other persons, visited with the Pages. Friends and total strangers showed sympathy to the family. Letters and cards came from all over the country, and some even came from foreign countries.

In the article, Mr. Page expressed his gratitude for the kindness and support so many people had shown him and his family. He said that the goodness of people comes out in the time of tragedy.

As we got closer to playing in our first game of the season against Indiana University, Mr. Page visited our practice field and told us not to let Greg's injury slow us down. He wanted to encourage us and show everyone that he had no ill feelings. That took real strength and fortitude. Mr. and Mrs. Page were people of great character.

McGill said Coach Bradshaw was permitted in Greg's intensive-care room daily and would keep him informed of how his teammates were doing and what strategy they were using for some of the games.

The first game in 1967 was against Indiana University in Bloomington, Indiana, on September 23. A number of newspaper articles came out in anticipation of the historical significance of that game and of that year. United Press International's David Moffit wrote a story that appeared under the headline "Kentucky Will Make Conference History: Wildcats Won't Be Contenders but Will Have First Negro Player." The article said that although Kentucky would not be a contender for the SEC championship, they would make history. It said, "They have the first Negro football player in the conference. He's Nat Northington, a 170-pound sophomore from Louisville."

In that article, Bradshaw predicted I would become the best defensive back in the school's history. That was a lot of pressure for a young man who hadn't played his first varsity game yet, and I felt honored, but it was bittersweet because I would have given anything if Greg and I could have been there together. I knew I had to go out there and give it my all because now I had to do it for Greg. Even with the bad shoulder, I was listed as the starting safety on the depth chart going into our season opener. The game was huge because not only was Indiana a border state but IU was a member of the Big Ten Conference as well.

The team took a bus from Lexington to Bloomington, just a few hundred miles away. On game day, both UK and IU fans came out to fill the forty-eight-thousand-seat stadium for this eagerly awaited game. IU's game program said, "Kentucky enters this game after a fall practice period that produced what veteran Lexington observers call our worst run of injuries in many years." Five of the top twenty-two players were affected by injuries. I was to be the starter at safety on defense, but because of my shoulder problem, I was only able to see limited action in the game on the punt-return team.

My appearance in that game made history. I was unaware of the historical importance until my niece, Ashley McHaney, an IU student, brought it to my attention. During a history class in 2012, she discovered that I had been the first African American to play in a game involving both an SEC team and a Big Ten team. She was very excited to learn that her uncle was part of history. I am proud and happy that she recognizes and appreciates what Greg, I, and so many other pioneers went through during these turbulent times for the betterment of our society.

Of course, the Big Ten had integrated years before, so IU's team had a number of Black players. In fact, we lost the game when one of IU's Black players, tight end Al Gage, grabbed a tipped pass in the end zone for the touchdown that gave his team a 12–10 victory. It was disappointing to lose the game that way. IU had an outstanding team that year, and it was a hard-fought game. They used the game as a springboard and went on to tie for the Big Ten championship. The Hoosiers made one of their rare appearances in the Rose Bowl game in Pasadena, California. After the game, I could not help but think, "What if I did not have the shoulder injury?" Maybe I could have intercepted that pass in the end zone or knocked it down. It was just one of those bad breaks, and we certainly had our share of those. What if Greg had been there and been able to play? We might have made enough of a difference to help our team pull out a victory.

As the team made the long ride back to Lexington, everyone was quiet and dejected. I was especially down, thinking about whether things would ever change for Greg. For now I would be going back to my empty dorm room, attending practice, and praying for the best.

I was hoping my shoulder would improve so I would be ready for the Ole Miss game coming up at home the following week. It would be my first game against an SEC opponent, the opportunity to break the color barrier, but I can't say that was my main motivation. My main objective, like that of any other athlete, was to give 110 percent and play the way I knew I was capable of playing. I was confident in my ability, if only I could stay healthy. For an athlete, it is extremely difficult to watch your teammates giving everything they have and leaving everything on the field when you know that you could make a difference but you can't play. I knew I could help the team if I could just get in the game and if my shoulder would hold up. If things did not improve, what else could possibly happen?

After all we had been through—the long freshman year, summer school, Greg's injury, and my injuries—I was definitely ready to play, and for a better outcome. On the day before the Mississippi game, however, things changed for the worse.

Greg's condition had continued to worsen, but it seemed to improve somewhat the day before the home game against Ole Miss, scheduled for September 30, 1967. He even asked to watch his TV for the first time in about a week. However, this would only last for a moment. Greg passed away that night, on September 29, 1967, after thirty-eight days in the hospital. We found out from Coach Bradshaw when he awakened us early on Saturday morning to give us the news that Greg was gone. It was a devastating blow, so much so that I still cannot fully explain the way I felt at that moment. A flood of emotion rose up inside, and it was like someone had thrown a wet blanket over my head. It was as though the weight of the whole world had just come down on me. Greg had become like a brother to me, and now he was gone. However, I knew he would not have to suffer anymore, and being a man of faith, I knew he was in the hands of a just God. At that moment, breaking the color barrier, along with everything else, was the furthest thing from my mind. Even today I cannot put into words the pain I felt after Greg's death.

After the initial shock, my thoughts and concerns were for Greg's parents and his two brothers, Charles and Robert Melvin. I had met them, and Greg had talked about them all the time. He had really loved his family. I could not even imagine the pain and sorrow they must have been going through. My prayers and sympathy went out to them.

Coach Bradshaw explained to us that the game against Ole Miss would go on at the request of Greg's parents. Although I was left to go on and integrate SEC football alone, I did not play a single game without him. Greg Page was there all the time, in my heart.

10

Breaking the Color Barrier

When I finally broke the color barrier, it was in front of our home crowd in Lexington, Kentucky, playing Ole Miss. I believe God worked it out that way. I did not have to go to Mississippi or one of the other southern states. Although we were able to play the game in my own backyard, so to speak, we were still playing against a team from the state of Mississippi. This is a school where the mascot used to dress like a plantation owner. From 1951 to 1966, Ole Miss had the best record of any school in the SEC (124 wins and only 25 losses and 9 ties, for a 0.813 winning percentage). That made Mississippi a more successful program than Alabama, Tennessee, Louisiana State, Florida, and Georgia.

It would be the first game between two SEC schools in which an African American played in any sport in the history of the league. I thank God for giving me the grace and courage that allowed me to be in that position, and I am grateful. If only Greg could have been there with me; in my heart, he was.

It was extremely difficult trying to prepare for a football game the same day someone like a brother had just passed. I had to get ready to play the game, but I was just going through the motions. I cannot even tell you what all transpired that day. It is like a fog in my mind. I tried to eat the pregame meal, but it was no use. I was just going through the motions of heading to the stadium, getting dressed, and coming out for warm-ups. I knew how Greg loved life and football and how he had looked forward to playing in front of thirty-seven thousand enthusiastic, faithful, screaming Kentucky football fans, especially against the team from his dad's and my mom's home state of Mississippi. Ole Miss would be the last school in the SEC to integrate its football program. That would not come until September 30, 1972, five full years after I played against them.

Throughout the day of the game, however, I couldn't escape the feeling that my friend Greg Page should have been on that field with me. After Greg's death, Coach Bradshaw said the university wanted to cancel the game against Mississippi, but Greg's parents insisted the game go on. They felt Greg would have wanted it that way. I thought canceling it would have been a great way to show respect to my friend, but I knew his parents were right. Greg would not have wanted us to cancel the game, and he would have been there cheering us on with that smiling face of his.

Physically, I was ready to play in this historic game because it had been several weeks since my last shoulder dislocation. However, mentally and emotionally, I was just not there. Because of my shoulder, I probably would not start the game, but I expected to see plenty of playing time. I would be at the safety position and maybe run back punts, if my shoulder held up. For history and the record books, it was a day filled with excitement and significance. For me, it turned out to be a day filled with mixed emotions and one that left me feeling extremely sad. We all wanted to honor the wishes of Greg's parents, so we prepared for the game as best we could. I tried to approach the game the way I always had, without thinking too much about the color barrier. No matter what I did, thoughts of Greg were right there.

As I came onto the field with my teammates, we received a welcoming round of applause. It made me feel good. It was like a fan had said in the newspaper when Greg and I played in the East-West All-Star game in Lexington a year earlier: "I don't care what color they are as long as they can play football." I knew I could play football. We had no way of knowing whether the fans were aware of Greg's death, but the announcer asked everyone to bow their heads for a moment of silence to offer a prayer for the Page family.

It was a pleasant, sunny autumn day, perfect for football. Fans filled with excitement packed the stadium. Once the game started, Ole Miss seemed to move the ball down the field at will against our young, inexperienced team, and things were not looking good. I was eager to get in the game, and it didn't take long. After a few minutes in the first quarter, the coaches sent me in. I did not feel any unusual nervousness. Despite the historic significance of that day, because of Greg's death, to me it was just another game. I had prepared for it my entire life, playing at the highest level I could. Now I was ready to do my job making tackles, breaking up passes, and getting as many yards on kickoff and punt returns as I could. I tried my best to focus entirely on my assignments.

When it came time for the first historic play, I lined up in the safety position, as the Ole Miss players came up to the line of scrimmage. The quarterback called out the signal, took the snap, and handed off to the halfback, who ran off right tackle and headed upfield. As a safety, it was my job to be in position to make the tackle if our first line of defense broke down, so I pursued the ball carrier to the point where our linebacker and cornerback made the tackle. I did not get an opportunity to get in on it, but I was in position just in case.

The next play was also a running play, but this time it was to my right. Again, I pursued and came up just as the tackle was being made. However, they were making too many yards on each play, moving the ball upfield toward our goal line. We needed to stop them at the point of attack, because it's not good if the linebackers and backs are making tackles five to ten yards down the field. Again, I lined up in my safety position and got into my stance as the Ole Miss quarterback brought the team up to the line of scrimmage. I read the play just as before as he handed the ball off to the halfback. Somehow he broke through our defense, and as he headed up the middle of the field, I was following the play all the way. As he darted speedily to his left, I pursued and moved into position to make the tackle. He had a blocker in front of him, and as they moved up the field, I could see the big lineman drawing a bead on me.

As I approached the runner, I broke down into my stance to prepare for the tackle, with the blocker approaching me. The runner planted his foot and made a cut back to try to avoid me, but I avoided the blocker and got my arm around the ball carrier's leg, bringing him down. As we all fell to the ground, my shoulder popped out of place once again, and all I could do was roll over in pain. I don't know whether the contact with the runner and blocker caused the dislocation or it happened after we fell to the turf. As I lay there, trainers came to check on me. Then, as I got up to walk off the field, I heard the fans give a sad sigh. I also heard some clapping as the other trainers and coaches met me coming off the field. I knew from experience that I was finished for the day.

Our trainer, Ralph Berlin, who was a kind and caring man, assisted me to the locker room under the Stoll Field Stadium and had me lie down on a table. As I lay there, making history meant nothing to me. All I could think of was Greg's death the night before, and now I felt I had let him down by being injured again and not being able to finish the game or to help my teammates and the team.

Back when I first dislocated my shoulder, I had thought I was feeling the worst pain imaginable, but the mental anguish that I experienced on this day was one hundred times worse. The pressure, the injuries, Greg's death all came crashing down on me. It was as if someone had thrown a heavy, wet blanket over my head. At that point, I broke down and cried. I had to let out the bottled-up anguish.

I had been alone on campus and on the practice field the entire time Greg was in the hospital. I had felt better then because I still had hope that he would make it. All of a sudden, reality set in. What would I do now after losing the person I had shared so much with during our historic journey over the past year? Although he had been in the hospital thirty-eight days, we had been there for each other and supported each other. How could I go on without that support? It was hard to believe that Greg was gone and that I would have to go on with the journey alone.

After the Ole Miss game, a doctor put my shoulder back into place, and I visited with my parents briefly before returning to my lonely dorm room. While doing research for this book, I came across an article on the internet titled "The Integration of Football in the Southeastern Conference" (May 9, 2012, on https://www.teamspeedkills.com). It noted that the day after the game, the Associated Press had written about it. The story went like this: "Ole Miss traveled to Lexington to face the University of Kentucky Wildcats. Mississippi overwhelmed inept Kentucky in the first half and rolled to a 26–13 victory."

The article noted that the AP report had missed "the historic importance of the game" by ignoring my role in it. The AP also did not mention Greg Page's death the night before.

An article in the *Louisville Courier-Journal* by Dave Kindred, published on October 1, 1967, did give history its due. It read, "Two UK players were hurt. Nat Northington, who became the first Negro ever to play in an SEC game."

I wish I could have played longer, scored some touchdowns, and helped my teammates win that game, but that is not the way it happened, and that is not the way God worked it out. Mostly I wish Greg had been there to play alongside me, but he was in my heart. My playing the entire sixty minutes would not have changed the historical significance of the game. History had been made. Integration had come to the SEC, and it would never be the same again.

With God's help, I made it through the night after the game. On Sunday, October 1, 1967, a memorial service was held at Stoll Field. UK president John Oswald announced that a Greg Page fund had been established in care of the *Middlesboro Daily News.* Dr. Oswald stated at the memorial: "The University of Kentucky is grateful for the time Greg Page was here. We are glad that his teammates and many other students had the advantage of knowing him. . . . And now we go on from the sober solemn moments enriched by this young man, his courage, his faith, and his short time with us."

The entire football team was there, along with Mr. and Mrs. Page. Two days later, a bus carrying all our teammates from our freshman and sophomore years traveled to Middlesboro, Kentucky, to attend Greg's funeral. Another bus of about twenty-five students, mostly Black, traveled there to pay their respects as well. That showed how much people loved Greg.

Years later, the university invited me back to be honored for my accomplishments. I had only one reservation. I told the officials that I would come if they also gave a plaque to Greg Page's family. The university agreed, and I went to the board of trustees meeting to accept the plaque. The university also recognized Greg by naming a dormitory in his honor—the University of Kentucky Greg Page Stadium View Apartments.

11

End-Zone Bleachers

When I thought about Greg's courage and the last words he said to me, I often found spurts of determination. I was ready to get back on the field and keep going. I returned to practice for the upcoming Auburn game, although I believe the coaches knew what I was going through and would have given me the time to adjust. After the Ole Miss game, I was very conscious of and concerned about my shoulder. As we flew toward Auburn, I remember thinking that if I even moved too suddenly the wrong way, my shoulder might dislocate again. Whenever I dislocated it, the doctors would just set it back in place. Since the trainers and coaches never mentioned having it fixed, I thought that was just the way things should be. I didn't know then that I had some damage to the shoulder bone and the ligaments that would require surgery.

Still, I was not going to let a little pain stop me from playing. I decided I would just play as much as I could, and if I was injured, then I would just come out of the game.

A week after my friend died and I was knocked out of the Ole Miss game with a damaged shoulder, I was on an airplane going to Auburn. My thoughts alternated from my shoulder to the tragedy, from the Ole Miss game back to the shoulder, and then back to the tragedy. It was a continuous mental cycle, flashing in my mind like traffic lights.

I didn't know it then, but this was part of the normal grieving process, and it was helping me to come to grips with my experience. Continuing to practice and play football was therapeutic for me, the best possible thing I could have done. Being around my teammates, coaches, and other people was good for me.

I remember that overall I felt healthy, but looking back, I know I was in need of some help to deal with the tragic event. I was in the most intense part of the grieving process. Just eating dinner and doing simple tasks that week had been difficult with my mind on Greg, his family, and everything that had transpired. I felt all alone every day after practice when I went back to my dorm with nobody to talk to and so much on my mind. Because of Greg's death and my injuries, I was also having a tough time getting motivated to attend classes. This would be a turning point in my career at UK.

Until Greg passed, I hadn't realized the full importance of his presence on the team and on the field. While he was there, I valued it, though I didn't know just how much it was helping me. Now, stepping onto a plane, into a locker room, and onto a field without him was awkward. I felt as if all eyes were on me. I'm sure that was the case. The coaches, the team captain, and most of the players were sympathetic to how I felt. They missed Greg too. The reality, however, was that he was not there, and it was time to play.

The Auburn game was not historic in and of itself, but I still think it was significant. It was the first time a Black player would play in a game against an SEC opponent in the Deep South. If that is not enough to cause some anxiety, I don't know what is. And for a young Black man in his second year of college to be going to Auburn, Alabama, in the middle of the civil rights movement was scary, to say the least. Today, many people I meet express appreciation for what I did and tell me what courage it must have taken for me to do it. Believe me when I say at that time I felt anything but courageous. I thank God he was with me. If not for him, there is no way I could have done it.

Auburn University is one of the largest colleges in Alabama. It started in the mid-1800s as East Alabama Male College. Auburn's record for the ten-year period was second only to Ole Miss's and was even better than Alabama's record. Under SEC Hall of Fame coach Ralph "Shug" Jordan, they had won 106 games and lost only 49. For us, that made it two weeks in a row playing against the two best teams in the SEC at the time.

For the record, all the teams in the SEC were outstanding in 1967. The SEC is a football powerhouse today, and it was a tough league at that time.

The league's degree of dominance, however, had started to take a downward turn. The combination of the other major conferences integrating, combined with the SEC's lack of Black players, contributed to this slide. The difference is that today, hundreds of African American players now dominate a league that—before I stepped on the field—had never allowed Blacks to compete.

Most vestiges of segregation in other parts of society had been outlawed by the late 1960s, but some of the folks in Alabama still had not heard. In his inaugural address just four years earlier (January 14, 1963), Alabama governor George Wallace had uttered that infamous vow against integration: "In the name of the greatest people that have ever trod this earth, I draw the line in the dust and toss the gauntlet before the feet of tyranny, and I say segregation now, segregation tomorrow, and segregation forever." It's interesting that part of the good governor's speech appears to echo the book of Hebrews: "Jesus Christ the same yesterday, and to day, and for ever" (Hebrews 13:8 KJV).

The same governor stood in front of the doors of Foster Auditorium at the University of Alabama on June 11, 1963, trying to stop four African American students from enrolling. I am thankful that he changed his position on segregation before his death.

In 1967, when we arrived at the hotel in Auburn, Alabama, I discovered that the team normally did not stay at this particular location when visiting Auburn. The hotel where the team usually stayed did not accommodate African Americans. Because I was on the team, we had to make other arrangements and stay at a different hotel. Remember, this was after the passage of the Civil Rights Act of 1964, which made it unlawful to discriminate in providing public accommodations, but that didn't make a difference in Alabama at the time. When looking back on these times, I realize that in some sense, God was shielding me.

Auburn had a very large football stadium, Cliff Hare Stadium (Jordan-Hare Stadium today), with more than forty-five thousand seats. One of the first things I noticed was some old wooden bleachers behind one of the end zones. This was one of my most memorable experiences from that game because sitting in those bleachers was a small number of African Americans. Seeing them was refreshing, and I thought, "God is good, and he knows how to give us comfort and peace." I didn't notice any Blacks sitting in the regular stadium seats, and because of the segregated times, I am sure there weren't any. I couldn't help but think that in this huge stadium that seated more than forty-five thousand, the only African Americans at the game had segregated seats in the well-worn bleachers. I felt bad about how shabbily they were treated, but I was still really thrilled and comforted just to see them there.

Phil Thompson, in Chip Cosby's documentary *Turning the Page: A Look at How UK Football Integrated the SEC* (2012), stated that he remembers seeing the Alabama state troopers on the sidelines with Confederate flags stuck in their gun belts and hearing them use the N-word and say "kill." I do not remember seeing the flags or hearing the insults. Again, I believe God shielded me from witnessing all that so that I could just concentrate on doing my job playing football, and he put those Black folk in the shabby bleacher seats to give me peace.

We got off to a good start in the game when my teammate Dicky Lyons returned a punt for a touchdown in the first quarter, giving us a 7–0 lead. After a few possessions, Lyons was injured, and I entered the game to return a punt. As I took my position, I was very nervous. Here I was, ready to make my first punt return as a varsity football player in the SEC. As a freshman in the fall and during spring practice and scrimmages, I had returned several punts for touchdowns, but this was quite different.

In the past month, because of my shoulder, I hadn't done much in the way of running back punts in practice. As I got into position about forty-five yards behind the line of scrimmage, the kicker punted the ball, and as it came off his foot, I saw it heading toward the far sideline and away from me. I immediately ran in that direction to attempt to field the ball, and as it went out of bounds, I breathed a sigh of relief. It was good to get in the game and to get rid of the nervousness, but I was relieved I didn't have to return a punt on my first play.

Because of the team's first successful punt return, however, it seemed as though the Auburn coaches did not want to take any chance punting the ball to me. They instructed their punter to kick it away from me so I could not make a possible return for a touchdown. That reminded me of that first time I saw my brother play back at Seneca High School. The other team had done the same thing against him. Thinking about that gave me more confidence.

After Auburn came back and marched down the field on several pass plays to score a touchdown, the coaches sent me into the game as a safety. On the very first play after I entered the game, the quarterback immediately dropped back to throw a pass in my territory, wasting no time testing me to see what I could do and what I was made of. I broke on the ball as it headed toward the receiver. As he stretched to catch the ball, I drove my shoulder into him, knocking him out of bounds. At least, *I* was sure he was out of bounds, but the official signaled a catch. Upset, I jumped up to react to the call and briefly questioned it. My coaches did likewise, to no avail. In spite of that completed pass, the good news was that I had been involved in some physical contact and my shoulder had held up. I was happy and believed that maybe I could make it through the game without injuring that bad shoulder again.

On another series, the Auburn quarterback again dropped back and threw a long, deep pass into my zone, near the goal line. I read the play all the way and backpedaled to keep the receiver in front of me. I saw the ball coming, and I was in an excellent position to intercept it. I had it timed just right, and all I needed to do was jump and catch it at its highest point, but as I jumped to intercept it, the receiver bumped into me, illegally interfering with my opportunity to make the interception.

This was clearly offensive pass interference, but the referee only signaled an incomplete pass. I couldn't believe it. That made two plays in which the calls had gone against us—or should I say against me? After that, I knew what was happening, and I knew it would be a long day. Yet I was playing well and without injury, so I felt more confident and more relaxed.

After several more series in which I was not involved in any plays directly in my area, Auburn called a running play to my side of the field. As I ran to get into position to provide run support, the running back broke free and headed up the sideline to my right, gaining ten to twelve yards. As I moved into position, I knew that if I did not tackle him, he could get a long gainer and possibly score a touchdown. He was moving fast with blockers in front of him as I sprinted to cut him off. When I got into position, he cut quickly to the left, as I had anticipated, and I was right there. I went down to hit him at the knees with my shoulder and arm as he made his cut. I got a piece of him, and my teammates coming up from behind helped with the tackle to bring him down. It was a hard, solid collision. At the end of that play, I felt the pain of my shoulder being dislocated once again. I don't know how long I lay there in pain, but I had to come out of the game to have it put back in place. I don't know what was more painful—the injury or the fact that Auburn pummeled us and won the game 48–7.

We were now 0–3, and things didn't look promising for our season. It was obviously a long trip home, and everyone was downcast. I couldn't help but think of when this all would end. I was not accustomed to losing or being injured and unable to perform up to my capabilities. Things were really getting to me. Besides that, I had to go back to that empty room again when we got back to Lexington.

Later I found out that two of my friends, Will and Marshall Seay, had frantically made their way to Lexington to check on me after the Auburn game. In their rush to get to UK, they got a speeding ticket. Unfortunately, they were not able to find me. I was sorry they got a ticket, but I was grateful to have true friends who were concerned about my well-being.

Too bad they were not in Auburn with me. But in a way, God did have someone there looking out for me and comforting me—the Black folk sitting in the old worn-out end-zone bleachers who turned out to be employees of the university. God allowed them to be there just for me.

When we played Virginia Tech at Stoll Field in Lexington, I did not expect to play because I had not gotten much practice time during the week leading up to the game. After injuring my shoulder in the two previous games, I thought the coaches would not allow me back in a game so soon. As the game progressed, it looked as if I was right, but going into the last quarter of the game, the coach asked me to run back a punt.

This was big-time pressure. It was a close game, we were still behind, and time was running out. We had lost three games in a row, and tensions were high. The team badly needed to score if we were going to pull this one out. I wanted to do whatever I could for the team. However, it was a gamble to put me in at such a critical time since I hadn't played or practiced much after hurting my shoulder again. Injuries had depleted our team, and I was one of the best punt returners. If I could run the punt back for a touchdown, we would have a great shot at winning. In short, the coaches had little choice but to put me in the game.

Virginia Tech had the ball close to midfield, so I got in position around the fifteen-yard line. It was a booming punt, and I knew immediately it was going to be over my head. All punt returners have been instructed not to attempt to catch a punt once you retreat to the ten-yard line. You should let it go into the end zone, and your team will get it on the twenty-yard line. As I retreated to the ten, I decided to let the ball go, but unfortunately it did not go into the end zone, and we were pinned back inside our twenty-yard line. We were not able to move the ball out of our own territory and ended up giving the ball back to Virginia Tech. We lost that game 24–14.

I caught a lot of flak from the coaches because I had not caught the punt and attempted a return. It seemed that everything was going wrong, and I couldn't imagine things getting any worse. I felt bad that I had not been able to return the punt and that we had lost the game, but I had done everything I had been taught. I didn't think that the coaches were justified in their criticism of me. I went back to my room feeling responsible for losing the game. Unofficially, this was the end of my career as a UK Wildcat, but it felt like the end of the world.

About a couple of days after the Virginia Tech game, I believe on my birthday, October 16, one of the assistant coaches called and asked me if I could come to his office at Memorial Coliseum. I tried hard to think of what he could want. As far as I was concerned, I hadn't done anything that I should be concerned about, so I met with him. When I got there, he informed me that I would be losing my meal ticket as a disciplinary action for missing some classes. I admit I had missed some of my classes during Greg's stay in the hospital and after his death. As I said earlier, it was difficult for me to get motivated during that time, and looking back, I realize I needed guidance to help me deal with this tragedy.

The assistant coach told me I would have to make other arrangements for my meals. To be honest, I was taken aback. Canceling my meal ticket? I was on an athletic scholarship! I did not feel that I should have had to make "other arrangements." What other arrangements? This seemed unfair. Don't get me wrong: I know that attending classes is very important. But how did this punishment fit the crime? As he spoke with me and said maybe I could go to the homes of some of my friends for my meals, I realized this was the final straw. I had no family in Lexington, and I did not feel I should have to go to anyone, regardless of how much of a friend he was, to ask for meals.

I'm usually an easygoing person. I can get along with just about anybody because I try to look for the good in people. Even in the worst of situations, I try to see the positive without complaining. The problem with people like me is that others tend to take our quietness for acquiescence, but I assure you, it is not. Yes, I can put up with just about anything, but everybody has a limit.

As the coach spoke, I was saddened, but then indignation began rising within me. I had always kept quiet and just taken it for the team. And the team had allowed me to take it, but I could not do that anymore. It was all just too much.

They say hindsight is twenty-twenty, and I partly believe it. This situation caused me to look back over my career at UK, and I didn't like some of the things I saw. I had not complained—after our brief walkout—when the coaches reneged (twice) on their promise to recruit more African American players. I didn't complain when they failed to place me in another dorm after Greg died. I did not charge them with being insensitive for not giving me another roommate. I didn't ask for a roommate at the time, but even a white roommate would have been better than being alone. I gave them the benefit of the doubt. It never even crossed my mind that they might have been playing Jim Crow by segregating me.

I never said a mumbling word when they asked me to play in games knowing that my shoulder was bad. I was more than willing to play, and I didn't mind playing hurt. I took the pain and suffered four or five dislocated shoulder injuries. The coaches had not offered surgery as an option so I could regain my health and continue my career. At times, I couldn't practice because of the shoulder injury, but when it was game time, they called on me to play with the injury. Knowing I was nursing the shoulder mentally and physically, they asked me to return punts. In the Virginia Tech game, I did my job the way I had been taught, but we lost the game, and somehow it was my fault.

Still, I was not bitter; I placed the team above my own health and made the excuse that maybe that's just the way it was supposed to be. All I ever did was love the game, love the team, and give my best for them. This was the thanks I got. At the time, I did not realize the emotional impact these experiences were having on me. I only knew I felt isolated and needed to make a change.

I now know how Jacob felt when he looked at his life and the things that had befallen him. "And Jacob their father said unto them, Me have ye bereaved . . . all these things are against me" (Genesis 42:36 KJV).

After the meeting with the coach, I decided it was time to give up my scholarship and transfer to another school. I needed to start thinking about myself and doing what I wanted for a change. I went back to the dorm, packed my belongings, and let my Black teammates know I was leaving. They did everything in their power to dissuade me, but I had made up my mind, and they understood. They were ready to go as well, but I encouraged them to stay and finish what Greg and I had started. I had had enough and had done all I could. If the coaches were going to treat me like that, I could see the writing on the wall, and I could not take it any longer. Besides, Greg and I had carried the baton this far, and now it was time to pass it on to Wilbur, Houston, and Albert. I truly believed that is what God wanted me to do. I knew that they needed to finish it to continue Greg's legacy.

In an article by Alexander Wolff that appeared in *Sports Illustrated* on November 7, 2005, Wilbur Hackett related the story of me sitting in my dorm room alone talking to the bricks in the wall because the coaches had not given me another roommate and because no other players had offered me any consolation. My teammates might have been too young themselves to understand the help I needed to deal with Greg's death, but the coaches had no such excuse. There was no offer of grief counseling in those days. At least it was not offered to me. I just had to make it the best way I could. Looking back now, I still don't understand it all. I am just thankful God was in that room with me and those bricks in the wall. After I returned home to Louisville and the word got around that I had left, one of the first people to contact me was Wilbur Hackett Sr. The team had a game against Louisiana State University in Baton Rouge, Louisiana, a few days after I left. When the news media realized I hadn't made the trip, they also started calling, but I refused to speak to them. Mr. Hackett was very saddened that I had left, and he asked if I would go back to Lexington when the team returned from Louisiana. He wanted me to meet with Coach Bradshaw and Bernie Shively, the athletics director. He said he would go with me and do anything he could to help.

Naturally, I shared things with my parents and friends. Although my parents did not try to persuade me either way, I could sense their great concern and apprehension that I might return to play ball. I didn't have to sense anything about where my close friends stood. They let me know they did not think it was in my best interest to return. They even reminded me of how I had told them before I had signed that I was not going there.

Hackett says that when he told his friends in Louisville's West End "that he would be returning to Kentucky for his sophomore year, they looked at him cross-eyed. It was like, 'Man, you gonna stay where they killed Greg Page?' That's what the feeling was."

My close friends shared those sentiments. They felt that I had not been treated fairly and thought that if I returned to meet with the coaches at UK, they might persuade me to return. I told my friends that I was just going to listen and was not returning. They wanted me to come back and go to school nearby at Western Kentucky University, the University of Louisville, or some other school. They were not confident that UK would treat me any better than before. When I left Louisville to go back for the meeting, they were concerned and said, "We know you are going back, aren't you?" I told them that I wasn't but that I was going to show UK the courtesy.

I agreed to meet with the UK officials because that was the right thing to do. When I arrived at the athletic offices, the news media were already there and wanted to speak to me. I reluctantly agreed but said they would have to wait until after our meeting. Besides Mr. Hackett, the Lexington masonry contractor whom Greg and I worked for in the summer months, my friend Mr. John Wallace, was there. Mr. Hackett and Mr. Wallace had already met with the coaches and school administration about the issues that had led to my departure. They probably found out what those issues were because I had shared my concerns with Wilbur Jr., Houston, and Albert.

Coach Bradshaw began the meeting by apologizing for the way the coaches had treated me after Greg's injury and death. He said the coaches should not have allowed me to continue living alone, without giving me the opportunity to have another roommate. He promised I could have another roommate if I wished. He also admitted they should not have continued playing me with the shoulder injury. He promised not to play me anymore that year and to have my shoulder surgically repaired so I could get ready for the next year.

As the meeting continued, the coach said UK would make every effort to recruit more Black players. Although Greg and I had heard that one before, I have to admit the coach was saying all the right stuff. I thought, "Finally, someone is addressing all the things that have been weighing on my mind," and even the UK staff seemed to be paying attention. This was the kind of support Greg and I had needed all the time, but why did it have to come to this before they got the message?

They were pouring it on heavy, trying to get me to reconsider, and I felt they were sincere. With so much going on, I didn't mention the threat by the assistant coach to take away my meal ticket. I had made up my mind to leave, and any promise to reinstate the meal ticket would not have made a difference in my decision. The damage had already been done, so why belabor the point? To top it all off, the news media were waiting in the hallway outside the offices. They knew the coaches were asking me to reconsider my decision to leave, and for a moment I really considered returning to complete the journey Greg and I had started. When I was home, the decision to leave had seemed easy. Now, with so many people that I respected pulling on me, the choice wasn't so simple.

I asked myself a question: Could I be successful at Western Kentucky, where my friends were, or at some other school, like the University of Louisville, where my cousin Ralph Calvin was playing defensive back on the football team? I concluded that I could. Anyway, I wouldn't be the first player to transfer to another school. It happened all the time. Many players who had transferred from UK went on to have very successful careers at other schools. I was personally aware of an All-American, Dale Lindsey, who had left UK to play at Western Kentucky and became an All-Pro linebacker with the Cleveland Browns.

Even so, this decision was just about as tough as the one to go to UK in the first place. Ironically, Greg had signed to play for Western Kentucky and had considered Oklahoma before he accepted a scholarship to UK. Back then, the governor's appeal to me with the idea of making history in the SEC had been a major factor in my decision to sign with UK. He had urged me to do it for my state, for the school, and for Black athletes, so I had.

Greg and I had successfully accomplished our mission of desegregating football in the SEC, although at a terrible price, and now I felt I needed to stand by my decision to transfer, and I expressed that to everyone. I realized I was disappointing others, but I felt it was the right thing to do. I liked the things the coach had said and promised, but it was still just too much. They had done too little to fix it, and after all I had been through, it was just too late.

When the meeting ended, I spoke briefly with the media and tried to deflect blame away from the UK program. I told them that I had made a personal mistake going to UK but that race had not been a factor in my decision to leave. I said that the coaches had been fair with us and that we had been accepted as Black players. I also indicated that my injuries and the low morale on the team after five straight losses had contributed to my decision. I expressed my desire to transfer to another school to continue my education and career and mentioned the University of Louisville and Western Kentucky as possible candidates.

Later, after reading comments attributed to University of Louisville head coach Frank Camp, I did not think the football program was interested. In a *Louisville Courier-Journal* article a few days after I left UK, Coach Camp said they had given me a chance to accept a scholarship with the University of Louisville, so they would listen if I wanted to talk, but they would not approach me. I did not get the feeling their arms were open, so I never contacted them.

The *Courier-Journal* ran another story after the meeting under the headline "First Negro in SEC—Nat Northington Quits Kentucky Football Team." I didn't like the word *quit*. I'm not a quitter. From my perspective, I was just moving on and transferring to another school to continue my football career and education, but from their perspective, Nate Northington had just quit. From my perspective, UK had quit on me and given me no choice but to move on.

I had an opportunity to speak to Wilbur Hackett Jr., Houston Hogg, and Albert Johnson before leaving. They were ready to go too, but I told them they had to finish what Greg and I had started. Our work had been done, and it was now their time. I assured them that together, they could make it. I know it was not easy for them, but thank God they did just that. They competed and persevered in spite of death threats and discriminatory and hateful incidents. In an article published on the website KentuckySports.com (January 10, 2010), Wilbur Hackett and Houston Hogg recounted stories of the death threats they had received in 1968 before a trip to a southern state and their attempt to avoid making the trip with the team. They eventually relented and reluctantly made the road trip. That showed real courage.

There was also a fight at a restaurant where they were refused service in another southern state, and they endured verbal insults and racial epithets during other ball games in the South. Those are just a few of the things they had to combat as racial pioneers in the SEC.

To this day, I respect them and am proud of them for how they persevered and finished the race. I knew I had to encourage them to stay, mainly because I believed they would get more support than Greg and I had received. I believed that the coaches had learned from the mistakes they had made with Greg and me and that Wilbur, Houston, Albert, and those who followed could benefit from the experiences Greg and I had gone through. The coaches and the UK administration had not been accustomed to working with African American athletes and therefore had not given us the necessary support. We were no different from any other young men, and they should have treated us the same as they would have treated their own sons. Our needs were the same as the white athletes'; our standards were the same, and we needed to be treated the same.

In fairness, I don't believe they truly understood what we were dealing with. This was evident in the lack of sensitivity I received after Greg's injury and eventual death. Even after my own injury, I tried to go on without Greg. When the support never materialized, as much as I wanted to continue at UK, I realized the time had come for me to move on. How could I continue with them threatening to take away my meal ticket? It was bigger than the meal ticket, and I recognized the warning sign. I just didn't know what it was. Maybe, because I was unable to perform up to my capabilities, because of the injury, they were willing to let me go. I had given it my best, and things had not worked out. It was time to write another chapter in my life and career.

Let me make it clear that I have much respect for the Wildcats, the coaches I worked with, and everyone at UK. I remember reading an article that noted that after Greg's death and my departure from the team, everyone might have concluded that the integration of the SEC had been a failure, but that was not the case. History had been made, the color barrier had been broken, the door had been opened, and the SEC would never be the same. The integration of the SEC was and is a great success story.

The things God had in store for me after I left UK included a successful transfer to Western and much more. My best friend, Will Seay, was a student at Western. He arranged for me to meet with Nick Denes, the head football coach, and his assistant, Jimmy Feix, in 1967. Because of the NCAA rules for athletic transfers, I had to sit out a year before I would be eligible to play, and that was not bad because Coach Denes said that I would have the opportunity to earn a scholarship when I became eligible to play in 1969. By the time I became eligible to play, Coach Denes had retired and Coach Feix had been promoted to the head coach position.

Two months after I left UK, I married my high school girlfriend, Dollye, and together we moved to Bowling Green, Kentucky, where I enrolled in school and began working the night shift at one of the local factories.

In 1969, before playing my first game at Western Kentucky, I was given another opportunity to return to Lexington and play for UK. Coach Bradshaw had resigned, and the Wildcats had a new coach, John Ray, who was very interested in having me rejoin the team. He contacted me through one of his assistant coaches, Ron Cain, the old Seneca coach I had played against in high school. He knew my athletic ability and felt I could come back and help the team. Coach Cain and my old coach, Jim Gray, were good friends, so Coach Gray became the contact person between UK and me. I realized my opportunities to be an NFL draft pick would be better at UK and in the SEC, and I was definitely willing to give this opportunity every consideration, but my life had changed in so many ways and there were so many other factors to consider.

I had not yet played at Western Kentucky since transferring there, and I was not on scholarship, so I was free to return to Kentucky and take advantage of my remaining two years of eligibility. I felt honored to have the chance, but in the end, I thought it would be in everyone's best interest for me to decline the offer. At that point, my wife had given birth to our daughter Renee and we had established roots in Bowling Green. We were happy with the town, the school, the football program, and all our new friends. Before I graduated from Western Kentucky, we were blessed to celebrate the birth of our son Nathaniel Jr. as well.

By the time I started practicing football again, I had been married and working a full-time job for more than eighteen months. Not only was I heavier than during my playing days but I was also terribly out of shape. I started working out in the winter conditioning program, and the hard work brought my weight down. I had a good spring practice and ended up as the starting tailback. My first year was good but not great. The two-year layoff from the actual game competition had taken a toll on me, and it took several games for me to get rolling again.

One of the people who inspired me was Ed Diddle, the Hall of Fame basketball coach. We were in the locker room preparing to play Middle Tennessee State, and I had not been impressive in the first two games of my junior year.

Coach Diddle was sitting in the dressing room before the game, and as I walked by, he called me over. He looked me up and down and said, "Boy, if I was as big and strong as you, I would run over them boys out there, and nobody would be able to stop me."

Well, that was all I needed to go out and have a great game. I scored my first two touchdowns at Western, and we won the game. From that time on, my fortunes changed. I was back in the game again.

I have some excellent memories of my two-year playing career at WKU. One of my fondest memories involves my daughter Renee being at the games. From the stands, she used to lead the cheers with the cheerleaders. That may be one reason she loves sports so much, even to this day.

Probably my greatest football memory is that of the homecoming game my senior year against our archrival Eastern Kentucky University. It was a big game, as both teams were undefeated and a victory could propel us to the championship of the Ohio Valley Conference (OVC). Eastern had a great team with an outstanding tailback in Jimmy Brooks and a great defensive lineman by the name of Wally Chambers, who went on to play for the Chicago Bears. The game was a bruiser, with neither team giving an inch. Our team held, and Eastern punted the ball down to our twenty-three-yard line. On the very first play, Leo Peckenpaugh, our quarterback, called a fullback counter, with me being the ball carrier. We had run the play for the first time the previous game, and I had scored on a sixty-three-yard touchdown run against Tennessee Tech in Cookeville, Tennessee. It had been one of two touchdowns I scored that day to help win the game. What would be the chance of my scoring again with the same play?

We broke the huddle and ran up to the line of scrimmage. I got in my three-point stance behind the quarterback, and our tailback, Clarence Jackson (New York Jets draftee), lined up to my left. Leo took the snap from center, turned, and faked a pitch to Jackson, as I took a counterstep to my right as if I were going to be the lead blocker for him on an end sweep. That was one of our staple plays, and we had run it several times already in this game. But this time, I stopped, planted my foot, and turned back to my left, and as Leo handed me the ball, I surveyed the line to see where the hole would open. The play worked perfectly, and I darted up into the line as the blockers pulled and led the way. We completely faked the EKU defense, and I only had to shed one tackler as I burst through the gaping hole in the line and headed up the field. The EKU defenders were beginning to recover and pursue me, and I realized it would be a footrace to the goal line. I could hear the homecoming crowd screaming and cheering, and I thought, "I can't let these guys catch me."

I felt the defenders pursuing me, and in my peripheral vision, I saw a defensive back coming up on me from an angle. I waited until he got closer, and then I made a sharp cut to my right, setting him up for a terrific block from our split end, Darryl Smith. I turned up the speed as much as I could, outran the others, and cruised into the end zone, tossing the ball over my shoulder for a seventy-seven-yard touchdown as the crowd went wild. All my teammates and coaches congratulated me as I ran to our sideline. I felt wonderful. That was the first score of the game, and that got us going and propelled us to victory and the OVC championship.

At Western Kentucky, I played with Romeo Crennel, future head coach for the Kansas City Chiefs and the Cleveland Browns. Romeo had been an outstanding defensive lineman but switched to offense when we needed help on that side of the ball. He was a great blocker who opened many holes for me to run through. During my junior year, he was instrumental in my emergence as a big-play scoring threat. Romeo became a graduate assistant coach my senior year, when we won the OVC championship with an 8–1–1 win-loss-tie record. As an NFL defensive coordinator, he earned five Super Bowl rings (New England Patriots and New York Giants). He was a great person and a great teammate, extremely personable and highly intelligent.

I played for some other great coaches at Western, including head coach Jimmie Feix, who was a Little All-American quarterback during his career at Western. As a senior, I was selected as the Most Valuable Offensive Player for Western Kentucky and was named to the All-OVC team.

After my senior year, I decided to run track as a means to stay in shape and prepare for the NFL draft. I became the number-one hurdler on the team, even though I had not run track since high school. Not only that, but I had never run the college high hurdles before, which are six inches higher than the high hurdles in high school. The Dallas Cowboys and Washington Redskins showed some interest in me and sent scouts to Bowling Green to meet with me. In trial runs for both teams, I was able to run some good forty-yard dash times for them. One of the scouts for the Washington Redskins was one of my boyhood idols, Bobby Mitchell. He had played with Jim Brown with the Cleveland Browns before the team traded him to Washington for the draft rights to Ernie Davis (the Syracuse Heisman Trophy winner in 1961). The Cowboys and Redskins continued to correspond with me through letters up until draft day, so I was hopeful I would be drafted. I knew it would be a long shot since I had played in the OVC instead of the SEC for the last two years.

A running back in the OVC would really need to compile some eye-popping statistics to be chosen in the pro draft. As a senior I played fullback, which is primarily a blocking back. Even though I had an outstanding year as a runner, I had not generated the yardage total I might have produced had I played tailback. The scouts were looking for more. On draft day, no one called my name. I was disappointed, but I was happy for three teammates who were drafted: defensive end Lawrence Brame, by the Cleveland Browns; defensive back William "Jelly" Green, by the Cleveland Browns; and defensive back Sam Pearson, by the Cincinnati Bengals (Sam is the brother of Drew Pearson of the Dallas Cowboys). I could have signed as a free agent, realizing that some of the greatest NFL players were free agents, or I could have gone to the Canadian Football League to play for one of the teams who had contacted me.

After the NFL draft, and after I had graduated and gone home, I decided not to contact any teams to try out as a free agent. I needed to get a job to support my wife and two young children. However, as the summer wore on and football season drew near, I realized I would not be satisfied unless I gave it one last try before giving up the game. I contacted the Cincinnati Bengals after their rookie camp was over to see if they might be interested in me. The coaches invited me up to Cincinnati for a workout before fall training camp began. I realized I was not in the best shape, and my chances were very slim, but I just had to get it out of my system. I had gone to work in Louisville, and I had not been training because I did not think I would pursue football. I did not do my best when I went to Cincinnati's camp for a day, and I did not hear from them again. I did hear from some Canadian teams that year, but I was not interested in going there with a wife and small children.

In retrospect, my best opportunity to make it in the NFL would have been as a defensive back and punt and kickoff returner, a position I never played at Western Kentucky. It seems the coaches at UK may have known my best position for the team and for me as well.

God truly blessed me at WKU, and I have no regrets. The UK era had passed and with it, my best opportunity of being drafted by the NFL, but I moved on when it was time to move on. As the old folks used to say, I wouldn't take nothing for my journey now.

After receiving a bachelor of science in business administration from Western Kentucky University, I worked briefly in Jefferson County government as a personnel analyst. From there, I worked for several Fortune 500 automobile companies as a field representative in sales and management before returning to continue my career in government. I served as executive director of the Housing Authority of Bowling Green for two years before returning to Louisville as the regional director with the Louisville Metro Housing Authority, where I worked for over twenty-five years.

I am responsible for the property management activities of the agency, with supervision and oversight of nearly one hundred employees and millions of dollars of assets. I have been directly involved in the agency's multimillion-dollar revitalization of more than two thousand public housing units. This project has transformed complete neighborhoods into award-winning, mixed-income housing, enhancing the lives of thousands of low- and moderate-income residents. This includes my old neighborhood Little Africa, which is now a thriving community called Park DuValle.

I believe the Lord has allowed me to serve in this capacity so that I can contribute and be a blessing to the poor and underprivileged citizens of Louisville and the entire community. I am grateful to be able to serve those in our society who are less fortunate and those who just need the encouragement and opportunity to improve their lives. It has been extremely rewarding to help improve the quality of life for so many appreciative individuals. In addition to providing decent, safe, and affordable housing, we strive to help develop other areas of people's lives, which will help them achieve success in our society. Self-sufficiency programs, which focus on education (with more than one million dollars in scholarships for our residents), job training, budgeting skills, counseling, and many other life skills, are designed to help the disadvantaged reach their potential. I am thankful to God for giving me this opportunity to serve. It has been extremely fulfilling in my life and career.

I am also a minister, Sunday-school superintendent, and teacher at Newburg Apostolic Church, where I got my early start in Sunday school. It is my desire to allow the Lord to lead me and use me in whatever capacity he chooses.

12

Glory Road

In her compelling autobiography *I Shared the Dream* (New Horizon Press), former Kentucky state senator Georgia Davis Powers tells the remarkable story of her life and career as the first Black woman senator in Kentucky. Influenced and treated as a peer by several prominent leaders of the civil rights movement, Senator Powers was blessed to share the dream of racial progress and equality with several powerful leaders. In doing so, she helped pave the way for many other female and minority leaders. To be a pioneer is to touch the lives of generations to come with your actions.

Like Senator Powers, I thank God for being able to share the dream as a pioneer. Although some of my influences were famous or national historical figures, many were not. They were simple people from my neighborhood, the communities of Little Africa, where Senator Powers lived, and in Newburg, where I grew up. They were special places, villages filled with great people from both secular and religious walks of life.

When we broke the color barrier in college football, others were fighting the nation's civil rights struggle all across the country, at the negotiating tables where Black athletes were being recruited and at lunch counters, bus stations, and voter-registration offices. The students who had the courage to step onto all-white football fields were part of a divine mission, and they were unstoppable. We were there to serve as rays of hope in the fight to eradicate racism in America and in American sports. While the jury is still out on America itself, in the sports world it would appear that the mission has been accomplished. When God opens a door, no man can shut it.

"I know thy works: behold, I have set before thee an open door, and no man can shut it" (Revelation 3:8a KJV).

I have to say that the media and the sports world have been kind to Greg and me, whether we deserved it or not. We have been given many generous titles such as "pioneers of racial progress," "groundbreakers," "catalysts for a positive change," "trailblazers," "pioneers," and "notable Kentuckians." One sportswriter, Alexander Wolff, even included us in a list of those he affectionately called "Our Jackie Robinsons" in his *Sports Illustrated* article on November 7, 2005.

Whatever the individual sentiment may be, properly written history will record two important facts. The first is that Greg Page's and my pioneer work opened the door for African Americans at UK and the SEC in 1966. This culminated ten years later, in 1976, with the UK football team winning its first SEC football championship since 1950. The second fact is that our work also paved the way for Black athletes throughout the country in the years that followed, particularly those from the South.

The following players were the first to follow in our footsteps and integrate their SEC schools: Lester McClain, Tennessee, 1968; James Owens, Auburn, 1970; Leonard George and Willie Jackson, Florida, 1970; Robert Bell and Frank Dowsing, Mississippi State, 1970; James Hurley, Vanderbilt, 1970; John Mitchell and Wilbur Jackson, Alabama, 1971; Richard Appleby, Horace King, Chuck Kinnebrew, and Larry West, Georgia, 1971; Robert "Gentle Ben" Williams, Ole Miss, 1971; and Taylor Stokes, Vanderbilt, 1971.

We also paved the way for players like Condredge Holloway, the first Black quarterback in the SEC, and for Heisman Trophy winners like Georgia's Herschel Walker, Auburn's Cameron Jerrell "Cam" Newton, and Auburn's Bo Jackson, just to name a few. In an ESPN Film titled *The Color Orange: The Condredge Holloway Story*, Condredge Holloway, as the athletics director at the University of Tennessee (UT), speaks about how he makes sure all incoming athletes at UT are given a history lesson about the pioneers of the UT athletic program. He believes they must know about people like Lester McClain. I am hopeful that one day UK will have the same sentiments and educate all incoming athletes about the pioneers who paved the way at UK and in the SEC. Having a poster-size picture of me is a step in the right direction, but I pray that more will be done in the future.

I feel honored and humbled to have been involved in opening the door. When I think about what we were able to accomplish, it gives me pride. I use the term *we* intentionally because we were all in it together: Greg Page, Wilbur Hackett Jr., Houston Hogg, Albert Johnson, Governor Breathitt, UK president John Oswald, my high school coach Jim Gray, and even our parents and siblings. When Jim Gray was inducted into the Kentucky High School Football Hall of Fame, he said one of his greatest accomplishments was helping me integrate the SEC. I could go on and on because many other people in their own very important ways played a part in the historic event of breaking the color barrier in SEC football.

Anyone who has done anything significant in sports will acknowledge the inspiration and effect that others, including rivals, have had on their careers. In my case, I believe it all goes back to my roots, back to when Dad moved us to the Newburg community.

As a youngster, I had some wise mentors, and I played with great athletes and made good friends in the sports arena. I benefited from the work, accomplishments, and friendships with people like Mike Redd and Wes Unseld. In some way, Redd must have inspired Unseld, who inspired other young athletes. This seems to be the way it went with all the young players back in those days, with one player inspiring another, and so on down the line. I don't compare myself with any of the other players from my village, but I am proud of the fact that I am from Newburg and am affiliated with some of the great people who lived there.

During my senior year of high school, the University of Louisville, my hometown school, approached me. I made an official visit and attended a ball game as a guest of the U of L football coaches. They offered me a football scholarship prior to my visit to Purdue in 1965. I informed them I would not sign until after my basketball season ended in the spring of 1966. I learned some years later that my dad had really wanted me to play at Louisville. Since Dad opened the door for me, if I had known his wishes at that time, my decision might have been different. He was looking out for me and did not want to influence me. He left the decision up to me, and I believe it worked out the way God wanted it to.

I have always been a fan of the University of Louisville football and basketball programs. U of L was the only university in my hometown that played football. It had also integrated years before UK. Even though U of L had excellent teams, it was not in a major conference. As a result, the Louisville teams of that era did not receive recognition on a national scale as they do now. To its credit, Louisville had a longtime coach, Frank Camp, who was highly regarded because of his successful teams.

One of the first African American football players at the University of Louisville was Lenny Lyles, who played from 1954 to 1958. He went on to play fourteen years in the NFL. Lenny played for the Baltimore Colts when they beat the New York Giants 23–17 for the NFL championship in 1958. That game went into sudden-death overtime, and many people refer to it as the greatest football game of all time. The significance of that game was magnified because it was the first pro football championship game ever played on national television.

Lyles passed away in 2011 after becoming a prominent and successful entrepreneur in his hometown of Louisville. Another great player who came out of the University of Louisville was Johnny Unitas, the legendary NFL Hall of Fame quarterback.

As a teenager growing up in Louisville, I saw a lot of coverage of UK football and basketball in the media, and I followed it as much as I could. At first, all the games were aired on radio. I remember the Wildcats Hall of Fame announcer Cawood Ledford, who called all the games for years. Listening to UK football and basketball games on the radio, along with reading all the newspaper articles, heightened my excitement about college sports. I was aware that the SEC had no Black athletes. UK approached Wes in 1964, but I had no idea they would recruit me.

If someone had told me I would be the first African American to break into SEC sports, I probably would not have believed it. When I was a kid growing up, it never crossed my mind. Like most young boys, I always wanted to play in some big-league sport, but I had no aspiration to become a pioneer of anything.

Before I got there, the UK football teams had had some good years when the legendary Paul "Bear" Bryant was the coach. This lasted from 1945 to 1954, before he moved to Texas A&M and then on to Alabama. During

Bryant's tenure, UK won the SEC championship in 1950 and then pulled off a shocking upset of Oklahoma in the Sugar Bowl to win the national championship. Entering that game, Oklahoma had been undefeated and ranked No. 1 in the country.

In the early 1960s, Kentucky's football team had high standards and expectations. It made some strides to gain respectability and national renown. But, as is common for football teams, UK was derailed by injuries. A cloud hung over the program after the NCAA put the school on probation in 1962. An NCAA investigation that scrutinized Coach Charlie Bradshaw's Spartan training methods resulted in an exodus of players from the program.

The UK basketball teams dominated the SEC for decades and won several NCAA championships, first under Adolph Rupp and later under the coaches who followed: Joe B. Hall, Rick Pitino, and Tubby Smith, who was the first African American basketball coach at Kentucky.

At the time I was being recruited by Kentucky, history was unfolding around me. It was only three months after I signed (December 1965) that UK's basketball team played Texas Western for the national title. In that game, Texas Western made history by starting five African American players in an NCAA championship game on March 19, 1966. The game is immortalized in the 2006 movie *Glory Road*.

UK was still an all-white basketball team at that time. Nobody could have envisioned UK basketball teams today, starting five Black players almost every game and sending four or five players to the NBA every year. My family and I had met UK's legendary basketball coach Adolph Rupp in early 1966 when we visited Memorial Coliseum after a practice. The football offices and athletic offices were in the coliseum, and we walked out onto the sidelines. This same team would play for the national championship against that *Glory Road* Texas Western team. Someone in our party commented that it was probably the first time that an African American football recruit had ever entered Memorial Coliseum. I am sure that was true. Rupp was polite and courteous, but he did not say much, other than to acknowledge us. I never had an opportunity to meet him again.

Every now and then, when a movie like *Glory Road* runs on television or when a sports commentator recognizes me as the first Black football player in the SEC, I get a better perspective on my role in history. As I watched the 1966 Kentucky–Texas Western game on television as a UK signee and Kentucky native, I had mixed feelings. On the one hand, I wanted the Wildcats to win. On the other hand, I found myself pulling for those five young African Americans who were making history.

As Texas Western went on to win the NCAA championship, some people may have wondered, "What if? What if UK had gone after Clem Haskins from Taylor County, Kentucky, in 1963?" Instead, he starred at Western Kentucky and was an All-American in 1968. What if UK had signed Westley Unseld in 1964? Don't get me wrong; UK had a great team with stars like Larry Conley, who became an announcer in the SEC; Louie Dampier, who later played with the Kentucky Colonels; and Pat Riley, of LA Lakers and Miami Heat fame. What Texas Western did that day made everyone take a hard look at integration. Even Pat Riley acknowledged that Texas Western's achievement changed the sporting landscape of the United States forever and for the better. The history-making victory also helps me see that what I did changed the face of SEC sports for good.

As I was writing this book, UK had won another NCAA basketball championship in 2012, with Anthony Davis leading the way as the MVP of college basketball. The Wildcats, by the way, had five Black players from that team who were first-round picks in the NBA draft. Times really have changed.

I believe my breaking the color barrier at UK and in the SEC opened the door for other athletes from my community and high school to earn athletic scholarships to UK.

Recently, someone suggested that after watching my brother and a few others play sports, I too was inspired to play, and my playing opened up a type of achievement for many other players. If this is true, then the open door extended from the village of Newburg to TJ, through Seneca, and all the way to UK. The hard work and talent of one athlete opened the door for others to achieve success.

As the first Black football players in the SEC, Greg and I became the models of inspiration and motivation. Once the door opened, others from the city of Louisville and the state of Kentucky made their way through. Following me through the door to UK from TJ were Tony Gray, Ben Thomas, Walter Burks, Greg Bass, Cecil Bowens, and Elmore Stephens, the 1974

All-SEC, All-American tight end, and my brother Ken Northington. The Seneca players from my Newburg neighborhood who went to UK included Carey Eaves and Darryl Bishop, the 1973 All-SEC defensive back and UK's all-time interception leader.

Others Black players who were not from Newburg but who made it to UK included Louisville Male High School's Bubba McCollum, All-SEC defensive lineman in 1973; Louisville Eastern High School's Orville Carroll; Owensboro, Kentucky's Sonny Collins, an All-SEC tailback in 1973; and Franklin County's Joker Phillips, who became the first African American football coach at UK in 2010. Unfortunately, he was relieved of his duties after three seasons as head coach and more than twenty-two years combined as head and assistant coach.

Still more great Black players from other states came through the open door. These included 1976 All-American tackle Warren Bryant; defensive end Art Still, an All-SEC and All-American pick in 1977; and All-SEC quarterback Derrick Ramsey. These players led Kentucky to the 1976 SEC title and a victory in the Peach Bowl in Atlanta, Georgia. In ten short years, Kentucky football had come a long way to make it to the top, thanks to the pioneers who had given so much. We will always remember you, Greg Page.

13

A "Man in Motion"

Since the Bible says, "The steps of a good man are ordered by the Lord: and he delighteth in his way" (Psalm 37:23 KJV), I believe the path I took was the right one. God was there when I signed with UK. He was there when I was injured. He was there to get me the visit to Greg's hospital room. When I thought I was alone in my room, he was there with me, protecting me from my own thoughts, fears, and feelings. God helped me to find the courage, and he gave me the peace, when it was time to leave UK. I thought I was doing it for me, but it was not "me" time; it was God's time. My steps were ordered, and my life was changing, moving in the direction God wanted it to go.

In 1 Corinthians 6:20, the apostle Paul said we are bought with a price. Prior to that, as if he were speaking directly to me, he said, "Ye are not your own": "What? know ye not that your body is the temple of the Holy Ghost which is in you, which ye have of God, and ye are not your own?" (1 Corinthians 6:19 KJV).

I feel that this passage is for me; it describes my life and my story. I belong to God, and even the times when I strayed away from him, he was there, leading me back, ordering my steps. Life isn't always easy. Like football, it can sometimes be brutal. I'm thankful that all my life, God has been in the game with me.

If you will allow me to use a football term, I guess you could say I have always been a "man in motion." Let me explain a little further for those who may be unfamiliar with the game. In football, a "man in motion" is an offensive strategy that happens before the ball is snapped. Teams use it to force the defense to reveal some of its strategies, keep the defense from knowing theirs, and change their own game so they can get an advantage. By disguising the offensive plan of attack, motion is often employed as a means to produce favorable matchups for the offensive team. Have you ever seen that guy who runs behind the line of scrimmage as the quarterback calls the signals? He's the man in motion. One of the good things about having a man in motion is that it moves the player to another position and even gives him the advantage of a running start.

God was calling the plays, and while he was calling them, I tried to figure out how to work out his plans. He was calling those plays to give me a spiritual advantage, rather than allowing Satan to have control over me. From God's perspective, my life has never really been about football. He has had me running for my life in him. "Now whom you forgive anything, I also forgive. For if indeed I have forgiven anything, I have forgiven that one for your sakes in the presence of Christ, lest Satan should take advantage of us; for we are not ignorant of his devices" (2 Corinthians 2:10–11 NKJV).

This is why I am not bitter toward the coaches at UK. I hold no grudges, and I have forgiven anyone who might have wronged Greg and me. I am now on offense—not sad, not mad, and definitely not loafing around, staring at brick walls, and feeling sorry for myself.

It is the job of a man in motion to expose the strategies and devices of those trying to stop your advancement (the defense). Being a man in motion allowed me to advise Wilbur Hackett Jr., Houston Hogg, and Albert Johnson to stay at UK. God led me to take the more honorable route, as opposed to him allowing me to act or speak out of anger and anguish.

"Train up a child in the way he should go: and when he is old, he will not depart from it" (Proverbs 22:6 KJV). Our family had more in common than just athletics. We all loved sports, but after we became acquainted with Pastor Mattie Holland and the Newburg Apostolic Church family, we discovered a new love, one that was in us all the time. God, in his love and wisdom, had seemingly placed something in us all that ran deep, deeper than football, baseball, or any other bodily exercise.

My maternal grandfather was a Baptist preacher. Even though this was long before I was born, I remember my dad calling him "Rev." I don't know if his church experience had anything to do with it, but my mother was saved at an early age, and she lived for the Lord up to her final day. I do know Mom's mother was a member of the Christ Refuge Apostolic Church.

My dad's mother was also saved. She was a member of the Triumph Holiness Church in Louisville and a true and "certified" saint of God. Dad used to always recount to us how he had to stay late at church, sometimes until the wee hours of the morning, while his mother shouted and praised the Lord. Many times, he said, they left church after the streetcars had stopped running and would have to walk several miles to get home. We laughed with Dad about that story on many occasions. I believe those long hours in church were not in vain. Dad was also a God-fearing man who was active in the church at an early age.

When you think about it, it's very interesting how we all ended up in church, serving the Lord. I believe, as Mom used to sing, "He [God] was there all the time," from the very beginning, guiding our family to holiness. He was there, inspiring us to come to him and using each of our experiences with him to draw in the next person and the next. When I was in my early teens, maybe fourteen or fifteen, the Lord gave me a strong desire to give my life to him. Coincidence? I don't think so. All my brothers and sisters have been baptized in the name of Jesus. I believe that everything that happens is in God's power; therefore, I prefer to view my experiences as the psalmist did: "This is the Lord's doing; it is marvellous in our eyes" (Psalm 118:23 KJV).

Sports may have been my family's first obsession, but nothing runs deep like the love of God in the hearts of his people. We were all good athletes and great competitors. It was in our blood, but now we are covered by his blood. I thank God for leading the Northington family to him. In football, baseball, track, and basketball, we all competed and tried to be the best there was. In faith, we are all perfectly joined together on one team and one side, God's side. In him, we all flow in our different talents and skill sets, with no competition, no screaming coaches, and no condemnation, only holiness. Thanks be to God: it runs in the family.

"For bodily exercise profiteth little: but godliness is profitable unto all things, having promise of the life that now is, and of that which is to come" (1 Timothy 4:8 KJV).

As most young adolescents do, once I got to high school and became a star athlete in four sports, I began to slack off in my church attendance at a time when it should have increased. I fell in love with the things of the world that the enemy attacked me with, the many temptations associated with the life of a teenager, but I thank God that as a teen growing up, I did not smoke, drink alcohol, or do drugs. Like most young boys, I just liked girls. I also liked the soul music sounds of the Temptations, Smokey Robinson, the Four Tops, Otis Redding, the Supremes, and Mary Wells, just to name a few. I think you get the picture. I was often in a battle between my spiritual desire to be a Christian and my fleshly desires. Some of those things continued throughout high school and followed me to college. By the grace of God, as a young adult, I still did not become hooked on drugs or alcohol, but I still was no more righteous than anyone else was. The Bible says that "there is none righteous, no, not one" (Romans 3:10 KJV) and that "all our righteousnesses are as filthy rags" (Isaiah 64:6 KJV).

In college, I made mistakes, just as many young people away from home for the first time do. Yet I thank God that the Bible is true when it says, "Train up a child in the way he should go: and when he is old, he will not depart from it" (Proverbs 22:6 KJV). In spite of everything going on around me, the upbringing from my parents and the instruction of my Sunday-school teachers was always in me. Being away from home allowed the devil a greater advantage to try to tempt me, but God always had a place in my heart and mind, even when I was not living as I should.

Even though I was not where God wanted me to be, I knew that church attendance was important and that I needed to change my lifestyle. Many years would pass and many trials and failures would come before I would again become active in the church and turn back to God. Since faith ran in the family, no matter what happened in my life, it was inevitable that I would return to my strong Christian principles.

I was baptized as a child in the name of Jesus, but because I had been so young, I was led to do it again at a later time. Salvation is a personal thing, and I did not want to take a chance on something so critical.

I was baptized for the second time on a cold Sunday evening at Christ Refuge Church in 1981. The pastor was my uncle, Elder Louis Cochran. At the time, I felt that I needed to repent for many things that had happened in my life, so I did as Peter instructed those who had gathered to witness the outpouring of the Holy Ghost on the Day of Pentecost: "Then Peter said unto them, Repent, and be baptized every one of you in the name of Jesus Christ for the remission of sins, and ye shall receive the gift of the Holy Ghost" (Acts 2:38 KJV).

Just as this scripture promised, a short time later, one night in early 1982, I received the gift of the Holy Ghost. It was a Tuesday prayer meeting. Since I had gone to church for the very purpose of seeking the Holy Ghost and giving my life totally over to the Lord, I arrived early. I knew I needed to be saved the way scripture teaches. I had just recently gone through some devastating personal circumstances in my life, and I knew that the Lord was telling me to turn my life over to him and that he would set me free. I was ready to surrender my life to him. The Lord knows your heart, and only he knows when you have truly repented. Once you have repented in your heart, he will give you his spirit as he promised. When I arrived at the church for that prayer meeting in 1982, a minister met me and asked if she could help me. I said, "Yes, I want to receive the gift of the Holy Ghost."

Jesus tells us that without him, we can do nothing. He told his disciples, "But ye shall receive power, after that the Holy Ghost is come upon you" (Acts 1:8 KJV). We all may have a desire to do right and live right, but we do not have the power to defeat Satan without the help of the Holy Ghost. And we need the Holy Ghost to enter the kingdom of heaven. Jesus told Nicodemus, "Except a man be born of water and of the Spirit [Holy Ghost], he cannot enter into the kingdom of God" (John 3:5 KJV).

The minister I met first took me to a small room in the front of the church and asked me to sit. She sat beside me, opened her Bible to the second chapter of Acts, and began ministering to me. She asked me to read the first four verses.

"And when the day of Pentecost was fully come, they were all with one accord in one place. And suddenly there came a sound from heaven as of a rushing mighty wind, and it filled all the house where they were sitting. And there appeared unto them cloven tongues like as of fire, and it sat upon each of them. And they were all filled with the Holy Ghost, and began to speak with other tongues, as the Spirit gave them utterance" (Acts 2:1–4 KJV).

After I read that, she turned to Luke 11:5–13 and had me read that. It is a parable that ends: "If ye then, being evil, know how to give good gifts unto your children: how much more shall your heavenly Father give the Holy Spirit to them that ask him?" (Luke 11:13 KJV). The minister asked if I believed God would give me the Holy Ghost. After I answered yes, she had me go back and read Acts 2:1–4 again slowly. This time I barely made it completely through because the Holy Spirit was moving on me. However, the minister wasn't finished. She told me to read it again. The third time, I started to read slowly, but I did not make it to the end before the Lord filled me with the gift of the Holy Ghost, and I began to speak in tongues as the Spirit of God gave utterance. All I could do then was rejoice and give him the praise for such a wonderful gift.

The only way we can know that the Holy Ghost has been received into our hearts is the evidence of speaking with other tongues, as the Spirit gives utterance. When the Jews in the upper room received the Holy Ghost in Acts 2:3–4, they spoke with other tongues: "And there appeared unto them cloven tongues like as of fire, and it sat upon each of them. And they were all filled with the Holy Ghost, and began to speak with other tongues, as the Spirit gave them utterance."

In Acts 10, the apostle Peter was led by the Spirit of God to carry the gospel to the Gentiles. Peter went to the home of Cornelius, an Italian centurion, whom the Lord had told in a vision to send for Peter in Joppa. After Peter obeyed the Lord and went to Cornelius's house, he preached the good news of Jesus to Cornelius and his household. In Acts 10:44, the Bible says, "While Peter yet spake these words, the Holy Ghost fell on all them which heard the word." And verse 46 says, "For they heard them speak with tongues, and magnify God." After they received the Holy Ghost, Peter baptized them in the name of the Lord.

Finally, on the apostle Paul's missionary journey, the Bible tells us about the Corinthians receiving the gift of the Holy Ghost after he laid hands on them. "And when Paul had laid his hands upon them, the Holy Ghost came on them; and they spake with tongues, and prophesied" (Acts 19:6 KJV).

The Bible, the infallible, inerrant Word of God, gives us explicit proof that the evidence of receiving the gift of the Holy Ghost is speaking in tongues.

I started running for Jesus from the day that I was filled with the Holy Ghost. Many challenges and obstacles have come into my path, but God has always been there shielding me, directing me, and placing people in my life to help me reach my goals. Even before I received the Holy Ghost, people like my parents, my sisters, my brothers, Greg, my friends, my coaches, my mentors, Pastor Mattie Holland, and her son, Pastor Waverly Holland, were helping God block out negatives and failures from my life. I'm just glad that from an early age I took Dad's advice to follow my blockers.

Being the first African American football player in the SEC is a tremendous achievement, and one for which I am truly appreciative and grateful, but it is neither the biggest nor the most important thing that ever happened to me. Next to God, my family has always been my top priority. My wife of the last eighteen and a half years, Gwendolyn, a true woman of God, is the love of my life, and all our children, grandchildren, and great-grandchildren are extremely special, a gift that only God could have given. Gwen is one of the main reasons I am where I am today. She loved me unconditionally when I did not deserve to be loved. The Bible says, "Whoso findeth a wife findeth a good thing, and obtaineth favour of the Lord" (Proverbs 18:22 KJV). I thank the Lord for giving me my wife. Since I began writing the book, she has been the inspiration for me to complete it. There were times I wanted to stop, but she encouraged me to go on. I thank God for bringing her into my life. She was a true woman of God. "Favour is deceitful, and beauty is vain: but a woman that feareth the Lord, she shall be praised" (Proverbs 31:30 KJV).

Even while fighting through a life-threatening illness and many trials she was a real inspiration to me, showing how God can give you strength, peace, and joy in the time of suffering. She reminded me of another song my mother used to sing: "I Won't Complain." Seeing what she went through and how she kept the faith showed me that we should never complain. I truly would not be who I am had she not been my wife. I love her to life and I will see her again in heaven.

My children have always been the joy of my life. I thank God for blessing me with beautiful, loving, obedient children, and I cherish them with all my heart. I remember when the Lord blessed me with these wonderful gifts. The Bible tells us, "Lo, children are an heritage of the Lord: and the fruit of the womb is his reward" (Psalm 127:3 KJV). Mine have excelled in school, earning bachelor's degrees while raising their own children and providing for their own families. They have grown up to become productive adults, model citizens, and pillars of their communities. My daughter Renee has many years of dedicated service in the business world, and my son Nate Jr. served his country honorably in the United States Air Force and became employed in management for a major corporation.

I like to remember the many things we have shared through the years. I remember them growing up from little toddlers to become teens and finally adults who have given us some precious grandchildren and great-grandchildren. I remember the football games we attended at Purdue and UK to see my brothers Michael and Kenneth play. There were times we went to basketball games at the University of Louisville, especially when they won the NCAA championship in 1980 with Darrell Griffith and the "Doctors of Dunk." We were able to attend the baseball games in Cincinnati to watch the great Reds teams in their glory days. With Joe Morgan, Pete Rose, Johnny Bench, Ken Griffey Sr., and George Foster leading the way, the Big Red Machine won two World Series championships in the mid-1970s.

Of course, we shared many quality times together that didn't revolve around sports, such as the trips to Kings Island and to family reunions in Louisville, Cleveland, Boston, and many other cities around the country. I am especially thankful that my children were baptized in the name of Jesus at Newburg Apostolic Church. We have a wonderful family—full of children, grandchildren, and great-grandchildren. I thank God for giving me all my children. It is indeed a blessing.

The game, the history, the wife, the kids, the education, the career—all these things may have appeared to be first in my life. However, they are all second to the Alpha and Omega.

14

True Vine

Because of the popularity of college football and the historical significance of integrating the game in the SEC, it is not unusual for me to turn on the television and hear my name mentioned in a telecast. Many friends and coworkers also tell me when they have heard my name on various radio programs. You can go on the internet and see a reference to me as the player who broke the color barrier in the SEC. I have read articles that mentioned Greg Page and me, but many of those articles also implied that I would not talk to the press about our experience.

There was a time when that was true. Today, however, I am compelled to talk, and not just about my experience breaking the color barrier in the SEC. My life and conversations these days are not only about UK and my role in college football history but about my salvation and my ministry. As a minister of the gospel of Jesus Christ, I am compelled to preach the good news! Jesus said, "The Spirit of the Lord is upon me, because he hath anointed me to preach the gospel to the poor; he hath sent me to heal the brokenhearted, to preach deliverance to the captives, and recovering of sight to the blind, to set at liberty them that are bruised" (Luke 4:18 KJV).

My desire to preach came directly from the Lord, and he gave it to me in an unusual way. More than twenty years ago, I was seeking to get closer to the Lord. One night after a long, tiresome day, I fell asleep on the living room sofa. Around two or three o'clock in the morning, I was sleeping soundly, when suddenly, I heard a voice calling out.

It was very clear and distinct but also a little odd. The voice said, "Nathan!" Nobody that I knew at that time had ever called me by that name. I don't know if I was awake or asleep, but as I lay there, the voice came again, saying, "Nathan!" This time I lifted myself slightly. I looked around drowsily to see if somebody in the house was calling me, but as far as I could tell, everyone in the house was asleep.

I had heard stories of God waking people up early in the morning and giving them messages. I wasn't always convinced, however, that this type of thing happened the way that people explained it. Now it was my turn. I have no other explanation except to tell you God spoke to me that morning. I am sure of it. I could sense a divine presence in my midst as I heard a form of my name being called out. No human being I knew of had ever addressed me by that name. Who would call me Nathan?

In the Bible, the prophet Nathan lived during the reign of King David and King Solomon. In the Hebrew language, the name Nathan means "God has given" or "gift of God." Jesus also had an apostle named Bartholomew, which is a variation of the name Nathaniel.

"Jesus saw Nathanael coming to him, and saith of him, Behold an Israelite indeed, in whom is no guile! Nathanael saith unto him, Whence knowest thou me? Jesus answered and said unto him, Before that Philip called thee, when thou wast under the fig tree, I saw thee. Nathanael answered and saith unto him, Rabbi, thou art the Son of God; thou art the King of Israel" (John 1:47–49 KJV).

That morning I had heard the voice of God calling me. The Lord was giving me the clear impression that he was calling me to a mission. A short time after this encounter, I attended a church revival. The evangelist was from out of town and seemed to be speaking directly to me. She said things that I had been feeling and that only God knew. I had never met this minister before, so I could not imagine how she could have known anything about me. She read the following scriptures.

I AM the true vine, and my Father is the husbandman. Every branch in me that beareth not fruit he taketh away: and every branch that beareth fruit, he purgeth it, that it may bring forth more fruit. Now ye are clean through the word which I have spoken unto you. Abide in me, and I in you. As the branch cannot bear fruit of itself, except it abide in the vine; no more can ye, except ye abide in me. I am the vine, ye are the branches: He that abideth in me, and I in him, the same bringeth forth much fruit: for without me ye can do nothing. If a man abide not in me, he is cast forth as a branch, and is withered; and men gather them, and cast them into the fire, and they are burned. If ye abide in me, and my words abide in you, ye shall ask what ye will, and it shall be done unto you. Herein is my Father glorified, that ye bear much fruit; so shall ye be my disciples. . . . Ye have not chosen me, but I have chosen you, and ordained you, that ye should go and bring forth fruit, and that your fruit should remain: that whatsoever ye shall ask of the Father in my name, he may give it you. (John 15:1–8, 16 KJV)

The message and Word of God convicted my heart. I knew God had my number! After the sermon, I got on my knees and sought the Lord with all my heart. That night I felt the spirit of God come over me.

I told the Lord I would do whatever he wanted me to do. I knew he was calling me to the ministry. Those two experiences of hearing God speak directly to me changed my life forever. Remember, I came from a family that is no stranger to church and ministering. I had always been impressed with the work of the preachers in our family and in my life. Still, I did not have any particular aspiration of becoming one.

After I received God's call, I became more dedicated to the church and to the ministry. I served as a Sunday-school teacher for several years before becoming the Sunday-school superintendent. I was in that position when God moved me to announce my calling to the ministry.

I was happy being a Sunday-school superintendent, but God had other plans for me.

What I didn't realize is that I was still a man in motion. God had brought me a mighty long way. He started me out running at UK, but those experiences were all for a reason. God used them to prepare me for today. He made me a forerunner of race and integration in the SEC so I could be a Christian forerunner for people of all races. He nurtured me through tough times and made me prove to myself that I could keep moving no matter the circumstances and obstacles.

I'm honored that God called me out of sin and shame and even called me out by name. He called me, inspired me, and just plain put it in my heart to preach the gospel. Now my mission is to run and tell everyone I meet about the love and grace of Jesus Christ. I am a true and living witness that you can make it, no matter what you are going through, no matter how lonely you feel, and regardless of who has left you or is no longer in your life.

If you allow God to call the plays, you can reach your goals. Years after your greatest pain has passed, you can look back and not only cherish your journey but also smile when friends, old and new, ask, "What have you been up to?" You can look them directly in the eye and say, "I'm still running!"

Conclusion

Endgame

I cherish every one of my childhood and college memories: the teachers, coaches, professors, and family, the friends, the struggles, the wins, and the losses. I seem to remember them all. Time moves on, but the most important memories linger for as long as we cherish them. Most are grand, some are not, but all are mine.

Physically, the Newburg kids have all grown up. Some have even gone on to be with the Lord. I hope those who are still able will make time every now and then to remember the good times: the times that made us think, the times that made us mature, and the times that made us laugh. One of my main purposes for writing my story is to share fond memories of the individuals, places, and things I never want to forget.

Will Seay, my best friend, suddenly passed away while I was writing this book. Will had been a tremendous inspiration to me since we became friends at the age of eight. He was a great mentor and my strongest supporter—in elementary school, in high school, and while I was at UK and Western Kentucky University. I could always go to him when I needed to talk. He was a tremendous speaker who possessed a wealth of wisdom, but he was also an excellent listener. He always had my back, and I always had his. Will went to the Western Kentucky football coaches when he knew I wanted to transfer from UK. He hired me at the housing authority after I became disillusioned with the corporate world and decided to return to work in the public sector.

Will was a spiritual man who loved the Lord Jesus Christ; his wife, Carol; his children, Stacy and Will "Mick" Jr.; his grandson, John Ervin; and of course his siblings, Rosa Etta, Fletcher Jr., Marshall, Artis, and Anthony. He made us—family, friends, church members, and coworkers—feel as though each of us was his best friend. He was a big man in stature, with an even bigger heart, a true gentle giant who would do just about anything for anyone. I owe a debt of gratitude to my good friend. He was a tremendous influence in my life and a man who exhibited outstanding character. Will had an unbelievable memory, and he loved to remind me of various experiences we'd had as kids and young adults.

He always encouraged me to write a book and was excited when I first informed him I had started writing my story. He offered many ideas for the book, and I relied on him for advice. He advised me to make sure I included the time when he saw the governor's limo driving down my bumpy street, taking me home after my visit to the governor's mansion. We had a good laugh about that. He was a man who believed in laughter for the soul, and he could make all of us laugh.

Not only was he proud of my historical accomplishment but he celebrated the achievements of all his family, friends, and associates. He was a great competitor who challenged everyone to always strive for excellence.

He deserves most of the credit for not letting UK or the local news media forget my role in integrating the SEC; he wrote to both organizations and led the charge for UK to recognize me with a resolution. He also headed the campaign to get the *Courier-Journal* to run an article in the newspaper during Black History Month in 2010 to recognize my breaking the SEC color barrier.

I am grateful to the Louisville Metro Housing Authority commissioners—led by Manfred Reid Sr., board chairman, and Tim Barry, executive director—for honoring his legacy by naming a residential and office building after this dedicated employee.

I will truly miss my good friend and brother. God bless you, Will E. Seay.

I will always remember the days Greg Page and I shared at UK as pioneers in the SEC. Greg was a strong, dedicated, God-fearing young man who left us much too soon. Together we made history, and he gave his life for the game he loved to play so much. He loved his family and his many friends from Middlesboro, Lexington, and across Kentucky. Although his time with us on this earth was short, he lived it courageously and to the fullest. I could not have accomplished what I did without his support and friendship. I thank God for allowing a friend like Greg to come into my life. His memory will always be in my heart. God bless you, Greg Page.

My life has been an unbelievable, incredible journey—from the day of my birth to this very day. I only wish Mom and Dad were able to celebrate and cherish this book with me. They have gone on to be with the Lord, but I truly believe they are with me spiritually all the time. Just as in the song Mom used to sing, "He Was There All the Time," they are there with me all the time. They raised me and my brothers and sisters in such a way that made my journey possible. They certainly deserve credit for the achievements, recognition, and awards that have come my way. Long before I broke the color barrier in the SEC, they were the true pioneers and trailblazers. They were born and grew up during a time of unbelievable trial for Blacks. They trusted God and kept the faith while fighting for their rights throughout their lives—especially during the civil rights movement. They persevered and never gave up, raising seven children to fear and honor the Lord. They were very strong, faithful people of God. I am a living witness to their love and influence in my life. I certainly could not have accomplished anything without their unconditional love, devotion, protection, guidance, and unwavering support. Thank you, Mom and Dad.

I am grateful that I had the opportunity to put my story in writing. God has brought me through the good times and the bad—times when the trials were so heavy I didn't think I would be able to go on. But God kept the promise he made to me when he said, "I will never leave you nor forsake you" (Hebrews 13:5 NKJV). I serve an awesome God. When I did not have the strength to continue under my own power, he carried me. He taught me that I could make it just like the song says, "One Day at a Time, Sweet Jesus." He put people in my life who were there for me, and he will do the same for any of his children. Thank God for all of you. We just have to trust and obey him. Without him, I would not be where I am today, and I would not have been able to share my story. As my journey continues, it is my prayer that my children will benefit from the examples in my life and realize that our Lord and Savior, Jesus Christ, can bring them through whatever they face in life. It is also my hope and prayer that everyone who reads this book will be inspired by the experiences found in my journey.

To the many football players and other student athletes in the SEC and throughout the country, always remember the pioneers who paved the way and paid the price for you to have the opportunities you have today. Remember those who suffered and sacrificed to make your journey possible. Remember and cherish the legacy of these courageous men and women, but most of all remember the one who gave you the talent and gifts you possess. They are truly the gifts of God.

In conclusion, let me say that this is not the end but only the beginning. The game of life is never over, even when life on this side is over. There will come a time when we will all have to face the reality of spending eternity somewhere. The question is where we will face it.

Let us all strive to make it to God's celestial shore—heaven—one day.

I beseech you to remember the words of the apostle Peter: "Wherefore the rather, brethren, give diligence to make your calling and election sure: for if ye do these things, ye shall never fall: For so an entrance shall be ministered unto you abundantly into the everlasting kingdom of our Lord and Saviour Jesus Christ" (2 Peter 1:10–11 KJV).

And finally, the book of Ecclesiastes instructs us, "Let us hear the conclusion of the whole matter: Fear God, and keep his commandments: for this is the whole duty of man" (Ecclesiastes 12:13 KJV).

As we continue on this journey, let us love one another and pray for one another.

May God continue to bless each and every one who reads this book, and may God bless our country.

Afterword

The story you have just read is true, but more importantly, it was brought to you by the living legend himself, Nathaniel Northington. For a myriad of reasons, down through the years, Nate shunned the idea of putting this story into print. Oftentimes, he viewed his accomplishment as nondescript, but the stores, libraries, and athenaeums receiving this edition of *Still Running* will relish the benefit of this updated annal.

Now at the fifty-sixth anniversary of his notable sports accomplishment, the additional light shed on his journey is sure to help sports history enthusiasts complete their understanding of the pioneer's chronicle.

An accomplished septuagenarian, Northington is not only maintaining his productive stride in life. To briefly iterate, he has been repeatedly solicited by major sports media to give interviews, to receive awards, and to take what could be seen as veritable victory laps. It has been a long run, but, speaking a bit tongue-in-cheek, over the years Northington's life could be aptly described as *déjà vécu*, especially considering the current racial and politically charged zeitgeist.

One of his favorite Bible passages, found in Hebrews 13:8, contains the words "Jesus Christ the same yesterday, and to day, and for ever." And with that faith operating in him, Nate Northington has not changed over the years.

Whether on or off the field, Northington has kept gliding forward past racial lines. As in the past, he has leapt the hurdles of pain from the deaths of his close sports colleagues and survived the emotional blitz of losing his closest loved ones. Southern sports fame and notoriety brought with them trial and trepidation. Despite this, Northington always remained calm, mustered up tenacity, maintained his momentum, and kept the faith to run past the walls of expected vitriol that loomed in his path as a Black player and sometimes seemingly the only Black person on the field or in the stadium.

In these latter days, the course of his life has drastically changed, causing him to run in a new direction. Despite being the consummate UK fan, Northington is no longer actively involved in organized sports. He is not pursuing touchdowns on the football field; he is an ordained and dedicated minister of the gospel. He has not, however, abandoned his love for his sport and legacy. He loves to reminisce and tell the story, but for someone who is passionate about racial justice and sports-related equality, it's often frustrating to hear Northington speak.

Either time or his religious faith has served him well. He's not angry. He has no grudge to hold or axe to grind against anyone of any color. In fact, while working on both editions of this manuscript, I was eager to hear him tell some horror story of animus or of being called the N-word or of being pushed, shoved, or made to drink from some separate water fountain. It never came. Whether he has long forgotten them or was somehow shielded from the terrors and frustrations of the menacing injustice that was certainly present in every step of his and his colleagues' journey, Northington has no bone to pick and not a single bad word to speak. To the chagrin of culture warriors everywhere of African descent, Nate Northington is a perfect gentleman. Perhaps his calm approach is the best. It certainly has merit, right?

The vehicle of racial equality is like a slow-moving steam engine. Yes, the train is moving considerably faster than yesteryear, and the landscape is better, but there is still a stench. The ghost of insularity past still looms across the path of equality and progress where race is concerned. This stench and those who generate it serve to sustain the overall racially stymieing effect that is undeniably seared into the collective consciousness of the American culture.

Today, even heading into the early days of the year 2023, we are still in a dangerous scrimmage to convince people that Black lives matter. Opponents of critical race theory, which has been around for more than forty years, still hotly debate it and dishonestly posit it as something new, evil, or anti-American. Nate Northington is an ordained pastor, a minister of the gospel, who survived the Jim Crow era and just happens to be Black. For sports enthusiasts, the good news is that *Still Running* is not presented as a book on religion or race, nor is it an attempt to fuel or refuel animus toward anyone or anything. It is simply his story, written with history itself as his coauthor. *Still Running* will not only inform but teach future generations that the train may be moving slowly but that the progress that has been written into history will not be forgotten, cannot be changed, and must not be ignored.

Making Black strides was challenging before Northington's college days, the same as they were during his heyday, but his faith in God has beautifully transmogrified his stride despite the loss of his beautiful wife in 2022. Northington is a man who was chosen to break the color barrier in SEC football because of, in his own words, him being the "total package"—having good grades, athleticism, and clean character. Some would arguably add that he was in the right place at the right time. The 1967 Kentucky running back whom commentators once described as "jumping and gliding like a deer on the gridiron" is now, in the twilight of his life, unstoppable. He is still jumping, still gliding, and, for his Lord and savior Jesus Christ, most assuredly still running!

Dr. La Monte McNeese
Apostolic Legends Archives
Clarksville, Tennessee

Acknowledgments

This book would not have been possible without the extraordinary support of a number of people. First and foremost, let me take this opportunity to acknowledge the one who made all of this possible—my Lord and Savior, Jesus Christ, for without him I could not have done anything.

After him, I have to begin with my wife, Gwendolyn. She provided emotional support and guidance throughout the entire process—from the decision to write my story until the completion of this work. When I needed help in any form or fashion, she was always right there for me. When I grew tired and weary and felt like I was ready to throw in the towel, she was right there to lift me up. She did all of this while she was going through multiple bouts of life-threatening illnesses. She never complained, and in spite of her own pain, suffering, and trials, she was there to encourage me to stay focused on the mission of sharing my unique and inspirational story. I am thankful and grateful to the Almighty for bringing this great woman of God into my life. The Lord chose to call her home to heaven before the completion of this revision of the book; however, she had assured me of her readiness to transition and encouraged me to be ready at all times as well.

I want to thank Dr. La Monte McNeese and the staff at In the Name of Jesus Publishing Consultants for your guidance and support in helping to make this vision a reality. Dr. McNeese is an extraordinarily gifted writer and a man of God who offered tremendous ideas and helped in so many ways that I never would have imagined. He brought some great ideas and substance to the narratives. And special thanks to Simone Cuarino, special assistant at In the Name of Jesus, for her perseverance throughout all of my changes during the process, She is a very talented and creative designer. I am grateful for all of your support.

I want to express my gratitude to my editor, Angela P. Dodson, author of *Remember the Ladies: Celebrating Those Who Fought for Freedom at the Ballot Box*, who worked tirelessly to help bring the book to completion. Angela was meticulous in every aspect and phase of getting the book into the shape it needed to be in. She is an incredibly talented and creative editor, author, and consultant who made a remarkable contribution in organizing and structuring the book. She also contributed considerably by suggesting many ideas that enhanced the book and made it more powerful. Many of her suggestions I never would have considered. Thank you, Angela.

I would like to express my sincere appreciation to a new associate and fellow football player, Craig T. Greenlee, the author of *November Ever After*, a memoir about the Marshall University football team's tragic plane crash in 1970, which killed most of the players and coaching staff. Thanks, Craig, for your outstanding editing, which certainly enhanced my final manuscript considerably.

I am grateful to Dr. Gerald L. Smith, professor at the University of Kentucky, for his support in the writing and publishing of this book. Dr. Smith has been not only a supporter but also a friend and adviser. His encouragement has made the decision and process of putting my story in writing much easier than it would have been otherwise.

Special thanks to my sister Rose Packer, an avid reader and writer who found the time to read my manuscript and offer many invaluable suggestions and corrections on historical events that truly made this book more appealing and accurate. She accomplished this while maintaining her normal schedule of reading several books each month. Thank you, Sis, for your contribution, support, and most of all your encouragement and prayers.

I am so grateful for the support and encouragement of my big sister, Barbara. She has been totally supportive not only during the writing of this book but throughout my life. She never ceased to encourage the writing of this book, and she provided many important details about our family and others in our neighborhood. She is a woman of God who prays for me continually and is an inspiration to our entire family.

I want to thank Robert Melvin Page, brother of my fellow pioneer Greg Page, for his support during the writing of this book. I am happy we were able to connect after all these many years. I thank God for you and your family.

Thank you, my friend Will Seay, for your friendship throughout our lives and for your encouragement over the years to put my story in writing.

Finally, I want to thank Ashley Runyon and all her staff at the University Press of Kentucky for your unwavering support. You have patiently guided me and supported me throughout the whole process of publishing my manuscript. The publication of my book was made possible by the knowledge, support, and expertise of the professionals at UPK. You all have been wonderful. Thank you.

Race and Sports

Series Editors: Gerald L. Smith and Derrick E. White

This series publishes works that expand the boundaries of sports history. By exploring the intersections of sports and racial and ethnic histories through the racial dynamics of gender, culture, masculinity, sexuality, and power as represented in biography, community, film, literature, and oral history, the series opens a new analysis of American sport and culture.